CENSORSHIP NOW!!

CENSORSHIP NOW!!

BY **IAN F. SVENONIUS**

Compiled with the assistance of the
COMMITTEE for ENDING FREEDOM

Front cover by Anna Nasty
Author photograph by Michael Andrade
Photograph on page 222 by Anna Nasty
Illustrations by I.F. Svenonius
Graphic assistance by Dan Osborn

Published by Akashic Books

ISBN: 978-1-61775-409-8
Library of Congress Control Number: 2015934075

Second printing

Akashic Books
Brooklyn, New York
Twitter: @AkashicBooks
Facebook: AkashicBooks
E-mail: info@akashicbooks.com
Website: www.akashicbooks.com

Ian F. Svenonius

Dedicated to M-26-7

Note: the backward messages contained in this volume do not necessarily reflect the views of the book or its author.

TABLE OF CONTENTS

PART I

CENSORSHIP UNTIL REEDUCATION

BAN
BURN
ABOLISH

1

CENSORSHIP NOW

WE NEED CENSORSHIP. Censorship to stop the radio from spewing its vomit nonstop. Censorship of the "free press," which creates a fantasy version of world events and the intellectual framework for mass murder. Censorship of the books that do likewise: hack, ghostwritten memoirs by political figures and celebrities who should be in jail rather than on the lecture circuit. Censorship of the film industry for churning out infantile, imperialist apologia and pro-torture pornography. Censorship of the arts, whose special status of immunity from culpability explains and excuses the degenerate ideology that makes all this "freedom" possible.

Indeed, of all these systems which require suppression and purging, we start with the arts.

Art is the linchpin. Seemingly inconsequential, "freedom of creative expression" is a red herring; a beard, a ploy, a false-flag operation. Upholding the inalienable right for art to be anything, say anything, do anything, is a parlor trick, designed by the lords of capital, with extraordinary, insidious implications. It has made art—instead of being the shield, weapon, and broadside pamphlet of the otherwise disenfranchised, attainable to anyone—into a holy bit of fluff, the well-being of which must be protected at all costs by the muscle of the militarized state. Upheld by the superprivileged, championed by the cosmically degenerate, what point is there in defending this beast? And what has the beast, in such company, become? Art is not purely sensual, nor does it lack intent or effect. Art is in the trenches, fighting for this viewpoint or that, either overtly or covertly. Art, in fact, incites more violence than anything else.

When the state, like a rampaging mob boss, systematically destroys its opponents (MLK, Malcolm X, Mossedegh, Lumumba, Salvador Allende, Che Guevara, Gaddafi, Fred Hampton, Orlando Letelier, Oscar Romero, nuns in El Salvador, untold numbers in Vietnam, Guatemala, Honduras, Laos, Cambodia, Palestine, Afghanistan, Haiti, El Salvador, Nicaragua, Cuba, Angola, Iraq, et al), how are we to interpret their patronizing embrace of "the arts"? With the regime reacting to its foes with such virility, how can the artist class not recognize the free reign extended to them as the ultimate put-down: the relegation of their work to sophomoric vanity? If art can "change the world"—which of course it can and does—isn't the "freedom of expression" doctrine really just a way to demote it to a theoretical gulag of absolute impotence and irrelevance?

Dictators from time immemorial have had dicta about what art was acceptable or not acceptable. It was a sign of respect to the role of art and the artist; an acknowledgment that art had resonance, meaning, and power with regard to international consciousness and ideological systems. Art lives on, after ephemeral political leaders, after the circumstances of its moment. It crosses borders fluidly, without visas or permits. It acts as a rallying point for generations; a totem of meaning, bridging the nuances of opposed factions for the benefit of a greater unity. Art serves politics as the "woods" in lieu of the trees; it provides vision, clarity, and idealism when one is bogged down by detail.

This is why it's a dangerous substance which must be regulated at all costs. Yet, as dangerous as it is for humanity, so is it a source of hope. If we believe, for example, that rock 'n' roll demolished the USSR and communism, as is more and more fashionable to say, then don't we believe rock 'n' roll—or some such art form—could demolish capitalism, a system wrought by even more contradictions, global discontent, and insane inequality?

Art, and so-called expression, must be placed under threat of censorship, with the means and the will to enforce it. For art to regain any sense of its place in the world, it must live under the shadow of the cudgel and the blackout. And not the passive-aggressive "market" blackout which is imposed on almost all artists. This is just a cowardly disguise for the ideological proscriptions of the ruling class. They demur to making explicit condemnations. We *dare* them to declare their objections, biases, and official censure of the contents of our records, paintings, films, and essays, instead of passively-aggressively ignoring them, shunning them, relegating them to the waste bin of penniless purgatory. Art is in a lost state now. It's a mess, without any idea of why it exists, where it's going, who it's for, and where it comes from. Censorship would immediately grant it a compass, a meaning, a purpose, a direction, give it its power back. An artist who is "anti-censorship" is essentially waving a white flag; declaring their work to be inconsequential; a smudge, a scribble, a doodle, or polka dot.

The music on the radio—pop, rock, rap, and country songs which promote class war and celebrate idiocy, sociopathy, immoral wealth accumulation, discrimination, and stultifying social roles—is the thrown voice of Wall Street. All of the broker's values are exemplified in this music. Regardless of whatever charm the pop star stand-ins may have, they are on the radio only because they reify the debased values of the sadist power structure. The elite seek to program, dupe, hypnotize, control you—who they regard as their property, their "bitch"—through these proxy singers. Censor them!! Don't let them talk to you that way.

Let them crawl collectively into whatever stink-hole they came from. They can perform in secret for the Walmart buyers' convention or whatever loathsome cabal of slime-pimps elected them to be the incessant, vacuous voice of mind control. But they must be barred from the airwaves, the record stores, the Internet, and public consumption. Censorship for the radio!!

The video games and films that the "entertainment industry" create must be censored. They are a virus unleashed into the minds of a nation; designed to cause violent, masturbatory passivity and to create absolutely obedient death machines. The liberal response to any contention that the stream of ultraviolence flowing from screen to eye to brain might be destructive is the following reductive equation:

"Shakespeare is good. Shakespeare's plays featured barbaric violence. Depictions of violence and barbarity of the most gratuitous sort are therefore not only edifying, but intrinsic to truly powerful art and part of a wonderful lineage which dates back to Shakespeare and the cradle of Western culture, the Greeks."

Or alternately: "Oedipus Rex was a disturbed individual who murdered his father, slept with his mother, and then blinded himself. Why is the *Call of Duty* video game, which trains its adolescent users to murder efficiently and indiscriminately, any different than a venerated Greek drama?"

Hacks in Hollywood, lacking the cleverness to write a decent story with poignant characters, churn out hyperbolic violence because of its sedative effect on the brain. The blood spills, the explosions explode, there is no gratuity left behind in the race to manufacture the vilest images and situations imaginable. The producers collude with representatives from the army, the navy, the DIA, the CIA; in short, the scum of the Earth.

They collect millions . . . and millions . . . from these tax-robbing institutions to tell their stories for them. Censor Hollywood. Keep their filth from the screens and their sad gigolos from the red carpet. They can engage in whatever pathetic rituals they choose; coital casting homages to Louis Mayer or bitchy e-mail exchanges in tribute to archdude Judd Apatow. But they must be censored until they learn to make a film with compelling content instead of relying on a mixtape of old songs to trigger an emotional response. Censor film and video now. Censorship until reeducation!!

Censor the news. Freedom of speech, freedom of press, and other media liberties have become a grotesque and deadly parody of their promise, with the "free market" ideology and financial interests determining their slant, their reporting, their "first draft" record of history. They explain the brutality of their insane system with a rationalized framework which at a distance would be revealed as absurd. But we haven't any distance. We are inundated, immersed, immolated day and night by the detritus that their free speech monopoly throws at us. A monopoly of power enjoyed by the most selfish, the most rich, and, therefore, the most grotesque and least compassionate. They have no restraints. They've gone mad. Censor them.

When the "newspaper of record" publishes a fantasy rationalization which explains the invasion of Iraq, an insane genocide, it goes unpunished. The press is "free" after all, free to spout lies and create war for its parent corporations and the ideological systems it serves. The seemingly inevitable events then unfold, while the journalists look on ruefully, *faux-naïf*, never acknowledging their central role in propagating mass murder.

When TV, radio, press, and Internet news are clogged with financial manipulation, reaction, and bile, can we believe in freedom of any of these forms? No. We must create moral restrictions on what is allowed. Censor the press. Censor free speech. Censorship now.

Censor the politicians. Elected officials, who are completely corrupt and sold out to the most putrid business concerns, are in need of a muzzle. Censor them before they churn out some more condescending, kitsch homilies to the "working families" and the "folks" who put them there. All they care about are the developer cronies and the whore-purchasing lobbyists whose asses they smother with love. Censor them and throw them all in prison.

Censor the technology. Technological "innovations" determine much of what becomes art, media, communication, and therefore life. We must manacle these mediums for the sake of expression itself. Why is industry allowed to pollute the world with whatever they decide to make paradigmatic through their control of the market? Why aren't there limits on these transformative technologies when so many degrade the Earth and our experience of it? Flat-screen television transforms every room and space into an outhouse, with sports matches and beer ads pummeling the passerby. Music, once a communal experience which bonded the listeners in a sublime and extraordinary way, has—through the introduction of "earbuds"—become a pornographic mind-control experiment, with tiny speakers transmitting awful boasts of sociopathy like a scumbag Iago, in order to promulgate a world where the most selfish act is compulsory, the most deranged attitudes encouraged. The sentiments expressed would cause consternation if they were played aloud. Let the truth ring out; censor the earbuds—now!!

Censor the Internet. The Internet is an out-of-control chimera. A pervasive, sicko addiction—worse than meth or smack or crack—which has rendered the entire population passive, fascist, and absolutely brain-dead. We need Internet rehabilitation for the entire world. Censor the Internet now!

These ideas are controversial, not chic, and even, perhaps, upsetting to hear.

After all, the modern Westerner lives a philosophically carefree existence. Largely "apolitical," he has few qualms about state violence and its use as a repressive force.

He ho-hums state sponsorship of terror, torture, air war, invasion, mass incarceration, and eco-S&M. Penetrations into time and space, as well as cosmic, cross-dimensional calamity are of no interest. Back-room deals by a syphilitic elite who sodomize the globe to quench their kinks are met with a shrug. *What, me worry?* would be their hue and cry if only they were literate enough to read *MAD* magazine.

Socially, topics like those above are in poor taste.

Off-limits both for discussion and private contemplation. Such esoterica is irrelevant to a life of Uber-ing to a Tinder date to share gelato with a prospective sex partner. Such metrosexual tomfoolery is never interrupted by political engagement except of the varieties which find play on social media: either outrage over the racist gaffes of political celebrities or semiotic delight on the implications of a hot cable miniseries.

This outrage, usually expressed online with an itchy index finger, is really a concern about social comportment. Designed to shame the vulgar or the gauche, its analysis doesn't extend to systemic critiques of institutionalized inequality or horror. It's just self-satisfaction with an "online community" about how "fucked" someone else is. Modern "social justice" politicking is, more often than not, Emily Post dressed up in some jargon *à la tour d'ivoire.*

Political engagement or activism is therefore rare but, when awoken, the West-person will spring to heroic action in defense of a few sacred values. There are certain "freedoms" which they cherish and see as indispensable to a fully realized civilization. One of these is a vociferous and wholehearted opposition to *censorship.*

For the Americans and their "First Amendment"—which guarantees freedom of speech absolutely—art must be free to say or do anything. This because the market teaches us that (apart from the possibility of fame and money) there is no meaning or consequence to art, music, or expression, except that it leads to more art and expression. Under their capitalist ideology, after all, everything is equivocal. All culture, art, style, and thought are just data to be absorbed and regurgitated on the radio, on television, or on a tote at a mall boutique. Che Guevara's beret, Himmler's haircut, J. Edgar Hoover's nightie are all postideological, reduced to design elements in a "melting pot" of projected profits and consumer caprice.

Meanwhile, "freedom of speech" (what they call it) is regarded as sacrosanct and no barriers can be put around "art," "expression," and the "free flow of information."

In fact, there is no issue which ties the Westerner's panties in a knot quite so much as the idea that "freedom of expression" is being compromised. Where did he or she get this idea that people should be allowed to say whatever they want? Would they agree to a stranger with a PA at their dinner table spreading filth and bile uninterrupted? Would they permit them to insult friends and family with a bullhorn for their "freedom of expression"? If society is a kind of dinner table, then the radio, TV, media, news, politicians, art establishment, tech sector, condominium developers, neoliberal think tanks, armed forces, and professional sports leagues are the dark stranger: taunting, lying, harassing, and inciting violence over the basket of rolls.

They respond that it's a two-way street, that we too can join in the conversation, and that "anyone can do it." This is another lie. Art and expression must make its case on "the market" to be created on anything other than a microscale. If the "art" or music, book, newspaper, etc., can't hit the charts, then it wasn't really very good, or so the accepted wisdom goes. The market has spoken. End of story. But in fact, capital determines success; number one hits are purchased, blockbuster movies are purchased, and electoral offices are as well. TV stations, magazines, and newspapers are meanwhile the party organs of the superelite.

The fake "market" is a de facto censorship to be sure, but a censorship which we don't control. It ensures a racist, militarized, idiotic, imperialist, paternalistic message permeates art and society. We need a people's censorship, a grassroots censorship, an insurgent censorship—one which doesn't rely on the hypocrite goons of the militarized steroid state or the esoteric Owl Club who run it.

We need a guerrilla censorship. One that starts from the people. A seemingly impossible or out-of-scale ambition? Not so. An avant-garde always guides the masses. The people's degenerate taste—sick and twisted to be sure—is a product of their disaffection from art, top-down programming, and the power of commercial psyop mind control. They can be guided out of the toilet just as they were guided in. We start the censorship one thing at a time, with a little organization, and a little bit of guile. We can do it. Censorship until reeducation. Censorship now!

The people want censorship. Their sadistic trolling on the Internet, the hate speech which litters the mouths of the lowest morons, and the massive popularity of pornography of the vilest sorts are misplaced attempts at being censured, whipped into shape, made to skulk into the corner. In the existential void created by the money god, any sort of punishment seems preferable to the asinine free/not-free purgatory to which we are assigned.

Likewise art—most recently rock 'n' roll—is always searching for censorship, nipping at the ankles of what is allowed. Such ploys are characterized as marketing stunts or infantile gamesmanship, but in fact they represent a desperate attempt at substance. Rock 'n' roll resents its official role as paragon of nothingness, meaningless rebellion to rehabilitate capitalism's predations and fascistic total control. It's always dreamed it could be something more, that its rebel gestures could be real. But the market denies it any meaning by refusing to censor its perversions, its provocations, its politics, or its puerility. His rights defended by the state, the rocker is reduced to nothing.

In lieu of the censor, the musical groups have created proscriptions for themselves by hiding outlaw esoterica on their products. Hence the satanic symbols in the designs of record jackets, the backward concealed messages engraved in the grooves of vinyl, and the tantrums thrown by the stars of the stage, who expose themselves publicly, break FCC codes, and otherwise pester the authorities to forbid their "expression." All to no avail, because the market's only meaning is itself and its own singular supremacy, which it pretends is "natural law" as opposed to an ideological or legislated construct. Its yawn is deafening.

These artists are looking in the wrong place; we need a guerrilla censorship which uses all the cruel tools of a revolution. Pain, terror, absolute mercilessness; not to placate some hypocrite Christian morality or idiotic social code but to stomp out the grotesque subliminal mind control and hate speech of modern culture, media, news, politics, and art.

The state can't be the censor. The state must be censored, along with its vile servants and its freakish masters. Censorship, termination, eradication, and liquidation.

Censorship until reeducation! Censor the state!

Censorship NOW!!

2

THE TWIST

THE SEXUAL-REPRESSION REVOLUTION AND THE CRAZE TO BE SHAVED

SAM COOKE'S SONG "Twistin' the Night Away" (1962) describes a scene where all ages, creeds, colors, ideologies, and class types are united in a utopian scene of unbridled excitement. An "older queen," a "chick in slacks," and "a man in evening clothes" all gyrate together in erotic abandon. They "lean back," "fly," and "Watusi" . . . but they never touch. Despite the optimism and joy of the tune, "Twistin' . . ." actually promulgated a new world of utter individualism and isolation.

Sam Cooke's song was one of many capitalizing on the dance megatrend initially announced on record by Cincinnati singer Hank Ballard and his group the Midnighters. Ballard's "The Twist" (1959) was indeed the first completely alienated dance form. Instead of being part of a pair, line, couple, or group, twisters were dancers who were liberated from stifling community; they were individuals. The twist was a revolutionary force in breaking apart social units and enforcing individualist ideology. Though rock 'n' roll music had existed long before this dance, the introduction of the twist was a shift which punctuated a profound new beginning for rock 'n' roll: rock as a culturally enforced paradigm, which cut across race and class lines.

Before the twist was introduced, a night of dancing, even if it were a wild folk, blues, or jazz affair, featured people dancing with partners, sometimes many different partners. Oftentimes, they danced very closely to one another. A dance partner was someone who was felt, smelled, held, and who moved in tandem with their partner's body. Sometimes there were dance cards issued so that dancers could reserve spots for various intended consorts. Emotional songs from the beginning of the rock 'n' roll era implored lovers to "Save the Last Dance for Me." The final cavorting of the night in the pretwist era, typically a slow and romantic number, was symbolic of the committed lovemaking of a partnership, as opposed to the evening's countless other tawdry "quickies."

With couples dancing, an orgiastic night of simulated fornication with multiple partners could be enjoyed by otherwise monogamous pairs who would lech the night away, their vows technically intact. Then the twist came in, permeating all social classes, propagandized into paradigmatic status with a hype campaign extraordinary even by contemporary psyop standards.

Pop envoys like Sam Cooke, the Isley Brothers, Gary U.S. Bonds, Petula Clark, Joey Dee, Chubby Checker,

King Curtis, Bill Black, Jack Hammer, Cookie and the Cupcakes, Clay Cole, El Clod, Duane Eddy, Al & Nettie, Chris Kenner, Johnnie Morisette, Danny Peppermint, the Troubadour Kings, Rod McKuen, and countless others brought the good news to the masses. French singer Stella satirized the ubiquity of the sensation with her "Les Parents Twist" in which she sang: *"How sad it is to have stupid parents doing the twist (while I try to sleep) / My mother has a fashionable haircut, it makes her look ridiculous / My father shouldn't have bought a sports car, it's hard to put all the family inside . . ."* It took four years of incessant propaganda for the dance to completely infiltrate all sectors of Western society, with "twist" records reaching saturation levels in 1962.

After the twist came other dances: the fish, the frug, the horse, the cow, the swim, the camel walk, the James Brown, the pop-eye, the disco-phonic walk, the monkey, the gorilla, the kangaroo, the drive, the funky Broadway, the cat, the fish, the bird, the tighten-up, the sophisticated sissy, the Philly dog, the alligator, the twine, the Harlem shuffle, the Boston monkey, the shake, the shimmy, the shing-a-ling, the boo-ga-loo, the bounce, the freeze, the continental walk, the slide, the four corners, the fishing pole, the happy feet, the mohawk, the pass the hatchet, the mashed potatoes, the fly, the popcorn, the karate, the African twist, the barracuda, the beetle hop, the drive, the waddle, the duck, the ostrich, and a multitude of other crazes or would-be crazes ensured the dancer would always dance alone (the Madison, which debuted in 1957,

NO--HE IS ALIVE...! MARK MERLIN... WHAT IS IT?
CHANGED! I FEEL INCREDIBLE POWER PULSING THROUGH MY BRAIN... GREAT KNOWLEDGE... AS IF I KNEW ALL THE RIDDLES OF THE UNIVERSE!

was different in that it was a communitarian line dance, as was "the hully gully" popularized by the Olympics in 1959).

The dances were a milestone in culture. Many were reenactments of animal behavior, such as the monkey dance where the participant acted out primate pastimes such as the peeling of a banana. With "the bird," the dancer flapped his or her imaginary wings. People were attempting to simulate wild beasts they had never seen or that were now scarce in an alienated, prefab world. In a sense, the dances were a funeral rite for a lost Garden of Eden.

With industrialization, humanity had realized its biblical prophecy and banished itself from the natural world, which it now only experienced through imperialist National Geographic documentaries. Food in the postwar period was, for the first time in recorded history, packaged without trace of its origins. Meanwhile, animals (except for a few domestic varieties) were unknown in the new suburban habitat. A few years before, pigs, chickens, and cows would have been visible within city limits, and butchers, fishmongers, and vegetable sellers would have plied their wares at markets. After World War II's corporate consolidation, food became something that was shrink-wrapped, freeze-dried, or instant and boxed.

Dancers furiously tried to embody the animals they could no longer see, in an effort to call them back—to express either their admiration or their jealous contempt for them in a bittersweet goodbye. Dances like the twist and the tighten-up were ritualized reenactments of industrial machines used in factory work. These were also vanishing in the new economy based on consumerism, wherein people's only skill and pastime would be to shop. All these moves were performed obediently following the barked dictates of a "lead singer," who mimicked the behavior of the foreman on the factory floor or a galley slave driver.

The new, individualist dance crazes were so exhausting—as well as psychically and physically devastating—that they lasted only ten years (1959–1968). By 1969, dancing was all but forbidden by rock bands who insisted that their audiences sit obediently and consume drugs en masse whilst trapped in enormous arenas, raceways, pastures, and superdomes. The rebellion of narcotics had the appeal of being hermetic, secretive, and illegal, but their real purpose was escape from rock itself, which had become intolerable. Rock 'n' roll's alienation had defeated its victims who were now rendered exquisitely passive. Occasionally, the trend for regimented dance moves would reappear—either as camp (the disco fad's "disco duck," the "Bertha Butt Boogie," and "the hustle") or as satire (punk's pogo, mosh, and slam)—but these attempts faded fast, impotently raging against the dying of the light. With the death of dancing, drug abuse became the rock fad, another step in the alienation of the music victim, lost in noise, buried in a stoned cacophony.

Before this, alongside the twist, oral contraceptives or "birth control pills" arrived, first marketed in 1960. The pill, though developed years earlier, had not made it to the marketplace, stymied by the FDA's moral and health concerns. The twist forced the agency's hand. Just as Adderall and Ritalin are part of a tool set required to navigate today's cyber-Internet consciousness efficiently, and increasing loneliness and alienation engendered by cybersociety create the need for pills like Zoloft and Prozac, so was "the pill" a necessary invention in the newly twist-ed world. The new paradigm demanded it.

The pill is widely credited for launching the so-called sexual revolution and for sparking a new era of promiscuity and rebellion against the nuclear family unit and its oppressive gender roles. But the pill and the twist, along with other postindustrial dances, didn't just encourage more sex without regard for pregnancy; they also parented a new relationship to sex. People engaged in intercourse with lots of different people not because they were newly carefree—there had been sex before this—but because dancing, the ancient ritualistic pantomime of intercourse and intimacy, was now an alienated action; an individualistic task where the participant was required to be alone, in a frenzied, masturbatory state, both highly stimulating and deeply depressing. The void was to be filled with actual fornication. The two phenomenon are therefore related: "The Twist" (1959) made the pill absolutely necessary, while "the pill" (1960) made the world engendered by the twist manageable.

Meanwhile, to dance now required working knowledge of new dance moves which—once the twist went sour—were always in flux. The discotheque was a place to announce one's adroit command of moment-to-moment consumerism. Dances were like gadgets or jokes which showed off working knowledge of temporal ephemera, leisure time (a requirement so as to learn and practice the new moves), and buying power (so as to purchase the records which were necessary components for instruction). At the disco, when the latest 45 barked out the contortion of the week, the dancer was ordered to comply with the locomotion, the turkey trot, the whatchamacallit, the choo-choo, the bump, the lion hunt, the "after the fox," the shotgun, the shake 'n' bump, the funky walk, the wash, the sophisticated boom-boom, the monster walk, the lurch, the stereo freeze, the moonwalk, the broken hip, the bounce, the weirdo wiggle, the squiggle, the Tennessee wig walk, or the pimp walk. One's dance partners were nonexistent or incidental; specters and shadows gyrating in the flashing half-light of the dance hall, hallucinations in the night. Sexual consorts were similarly identityless.

Sex itself was likewise extracted from what it had been—eternal and universal—and became a consumer's whim, a new move; i.e., "fashion." It was necessary for the rock 'n' roller to engage in actual sex because of the lack of tenderness; touching one another casually had been made verboten by the new dances. Therefore, the conceit of the sexual revolutionary wasn't only that those involved were having more sex but also that they had liberated sex entirely from its olden-days gulag of repressed courtship rituals and "teasing." A spate of tease songs (Cliff Richard's "Please Don't Tease," the Monteras's "You're a Tease,"

Bob Kuban's "The Teaser") appeared in the early sixties, bullying diatribes against "Little Sally Tease" (Don & the Goodtimes) and other women who weren't complying with the new era of mechanistic sex on demand.

Sex, during this so-called sexual revolution, was itself reinvented. Rock 'n' roll's stance has always been that it invented sex; that Elvis's shaking hips were somehow a revelation to all those who saw them, something altogether new. And they were. They were rejecting the sex of the past—the Lost Generation sluts and sleazeballs who cavorted, canoodled, and contorted with people like Fatty Arbuckle—to create something entirely different. Sex was redefined. It was an ultraindividualistic sport of play and pantomime which didn't even happen when it happened. Eros, once risqué, naughty, and discreet, became stark, narcissistic, and codified like the new dances; people practiced their moves, first through smut, then with post-hippie how-to manuals (such as *The Joy of Sex*), and then finally with "hardcore" pornography as a guide.

Pussy-eating, cocksucking, anal sex, threesomes, wheelbarrowing, and 69 were outlined, streamlined, diagrammed, and stripped of mystery. The cobwebs were cleared and a tungsten bulb was blasted at the newly clinical sex act. Without risk of pregnancy and with the new brutal aerobics of the frug and the jerk banishing intimacy, closeness, and tenderness, the teen-amphetamined world of rock 'n' roll begat a whole new scene. This started with the guttural obscenities of the first rock 'n' rollers. But though Elvis and other first wavers' gestural feats led the way, the twist was the coup de grâce which finally did away with the sexual tenderness of the old world.

New razor technology was also introduced in the new age, to address the compulsory youthfulness enforced by the new adolescent rock 'n' roll class. Formerly, "counter-cultures" sought wisdom and experience. The Beat Generation had wanted to look mature and rugged, while the Lost Generation were likewise scruffy adults. Now, people shaved whatever facial hair they had to maintain a young look. Not coincidentally perhaps, shaving technology became quite sophisticated in 1957—immediately before the twist appeared—with Gillette marketing the first "adjustable" razor, which allowed a closer cut than ever before. Yet all this shaving had another function as well: to enforce insensitivity, militarism, and a brutal machinist ideology.

Hair acts as antennae on the body. Hair on one's body makes one sensitive to one's environment. Religious people are typically hairy and resolve not to cut their hair lest their relationship with God—via their antennae—be severed. Hasidim, Amish, Rastafarians, Orthodox Muslims, and Sikhs all have edicts about maintaining certain hairs or hair that is sacred. Samson was the biblical story of a hero who lost his power by cutting his hair. Conversely, when the Greeks and Romans successively conquered their respective known worlds, they were remarkable for their decision, culturally, to be without facial hair. Lucius Tarquinius Superbus, a Greek descendant, was the last of the kings of Rome (535–496 BC) before the Senate era, and also the man to introduce the razor to the kingdom.

Lucius shaving himself signaled a paradigm shift which brought about his own defeat. The beard was a signal of the monarchic father authority, while the shaved face was androgynous and democratic. The razor excited new passions which struck with a dialectic fist. Shaving reversed time and blurred identity. Old could suddenly be young, masculine could be feminine, identities were revealed to be mutable/equivocal, and a craze for democracy was the result. Lucius's dynasty was overthrown and gave way to the senatorial Rome of historic renown. After he was deposed, the newly shaven Roman Republic was declared, which then set about conquering the known world.

The Romans had taken their democratic model from the Greeks of Athens, who had also been known to shave and oil their bodies, as had the Egyptians who inspired them. In antiquity, the Athenians maintained an empire in the Peloponnese, demanding slaves and treasure from their neighbors. The Romans eclipsed Greek conquests and have been the aesthetic template for most imperial projects since, e.g., the National Socialists, Bismark's Prussia, the European fascist movements of the 1930s, Napoleon (whose reign was synonymous with the architectural "Empire" style), Great Britain, and the USA (Washington, DC's neoclassical buildings, the eagle as national symbol, and the "fasces" wall adornment at the US Congress are but a few examples of the country's repetitive and unimaginative invocations of Roman imperial power).

Our sexual ideas are also borrowed not from the sophisticate cultures who created the *Kama Sutra*, but from kindred brutalists, the Romans. Roman depictions of sex in the ubiquitous brothels of Pompeii, which feature Priapus centrally, are curiously similar to images of modern pornography.

Hairless tribes were dominant over their hairy neighbors. Besides haircutting, rituals of self-mutilation were symbols of tribal potency; circumcision, an obvious example, was not religious but a cultural designator of toughness and exclusivity. In parts of the world with more history, such as Asia, it's theorized that relative hairlessness developed as an evolutionary trait of survival. As the Greeks, Romans, and Egyptians showed, less hair meant military prowess and dominance over foes. Hairiness was a sacred trait, reserved for the noncombatants such as holy men, poets, philosophers, crazies, and nursing mothers. Similarly, shaving one's body desensitizes ones body. It makes one more machine-like, more macho; it makes brutality easier. As soon as hairiness was associated with leftism, the fate of that ideological propensity was doomed.

With the so-called sexual revolution, people started shaving not only their faces but also their pubic regions. This began with an avant-garde of homosexuals but spread with the popularization of pornography via the Internet and the "hook-up culture" of casual straight sex performed by nerds and squares. The shaved body signals a person who's not hung up by attachments, feelings, romanticism, or any of the tawdry aspects of relationships or "love." The shaved crotch was one that was ready for wordless action steeled against vulnerability.

Onlookers of porn complain of the childlike resemblance of the shorn genitals, that the shaved vagina looks prepubescent, which makes them uncomfortable. But the shaved pubic area is meant to look preadolescent. It denotes a preadolescent disregard for the potency of sex in regard to emotionalism, romanticism, etc. Pubic hair paradoxically doesn't protect the sex organ but extends it; it is a quite sensitive part of it.

Chopping off one's pubic hair is akin to cutting the foreskin or female genital mutilation that persists in some parts of the world. It is designed to desensitize. Violence-worshipping youth cults such as the military and the "skinheads" of Britain typically shave their heads as a designation of sociopathic unfeeling. The hair, instead of protecting or hiding the organ, actually comprises thousands of feelers which lend sensitivity to the organ, exposing it to its partner's signals of empathy, love, lust, shame, fear, disgust, et al. A hairy body is simply less prepared for modernistic, mechanized body-mashing.

Hairlessness is an aggressive stance, and implies a lack of vanity and disdain for luxury. It implies a state of war. A French-style waxing job or pubic "landing strip" is like the so-called mohawk haircut favored by the Pawnee tribe and used in times of war by Cossacks, airborne troops, and the like. The "Brazilian" wax job is the full skinhead.

In the pretwist era, the dancer would often dance with many partners in a simulated orgy. It was essentially a tryout for sex or a replacement, but in its explicitness and its intimacy, it could not be called repressed. After the twist was introduced, sex repression saw its apex expression in the "mania" or alienated and displaced erotic cavalcade which met the Beatles and other stars of the era. After the disappointment engendered by the Beatles' breakup came a mass, culturewide depression. Soon afterward, drug abuse became practically compulsory for teens who liked music. This was another replacement for sex. The so-called sexual revolution, celebrated as a liberation which encouraged participants to have more sex with more partners, was actually a revolutionary transformation of sex: changing what had been the sex act into a series of alienated, self-conscious moves, or replacing it with the sensual high of the institutionalized "culture" of drugs.

3

ALL POWER TO THE PACK RATS!
IKEA AND APPLE'S WAR ON "HOARDERS"

I. APPLE VS. THE "HOARDERS"

THE APPLE IDEOLOGY is sleek and clean. It proposes a futuristic lifestyle without attachments or clutter, where mankind is free to chase down every desire, creative and otherwise, free of the "fuzz" of possessions. Like a nomad on the steppe, movement, horizon, and conquest are the only concern.

The room of the modern man is stark, but in its simplicity it exudes wealth and sophistication. There is just a bed or futon and an iPad. None of the old-time accoutrements which signified intelligence, artistic interest, or a curiosity about the world are evident. There are no magazines, books, or records anywhere. Just perhaps some high-priced "products," a.k.a. toiletries, in the bathroom. Everything he or she needs is on the Cloud.

Things, stuff, and doodads are just hang-ups, after all,

which serve to drag us into our past and harness us to prior ideas of who we were and what we are supposed to be.

The Apple world is apart from the old world. It is one where we can be anything, free of the wretched past. Just a being of light and electricity who wafts effortlessly from whim to caprice to passing fancy. Like their room, his or her body is also clean, shaved; streamlined for action. If one has possessions, one is seen to be rather fuddy-duddy and certainly not a sexually vital contemporary being.

The Apple proposition is a sixties futurist-Zen minimalist throwback, lifted from Scandinavian designers like Panton and Saarinen, whose Nordic functionalism was influenced by modernist movements like De Stijl and the Bauhaus.

While modernism proposed ways of dealing with the cataclysmic upheaval brought on by industrialism, Apple's proposition is the Western capitalist commercial: freedom, ease, sex, and cool control of one's environment. Apple actively encourages the population to lose their possessions. Music? Store it on the Cloud. Books? Store them on the Cloud. Film, magazines, newspapers, TV are all safely stored in the ether and not underfoot or stuffed in a closet. It's a modernist monastery where the religion is Apple itself.

Meanwhile, those who have hung onto possessions are castigated, jeered at, and painted as fools. The hit TV show *Hoarders* (A&E) identifies people with things as socially malignant, grotesque, primitive, dirty, bizarre. In a word: poor. Apple has turned the world upside down in making possessions a symbol of poverty and having nothing a signifier of wealth and power.

This is actually a bourgeois sensibility, an aesthetic of Calvinists and other early Protestants/capitalists. While wealth adornment was a no-no, extraordinary wealth accumulation was a sign of godliness and beatitude. These bean counters were pioneers of the modern aesthetic: owning things = vulgar; having obscene piles of money/capital beyond what one could ever use = divine.

The antistuff crowd invokes Eastern Buddhism and communism-lite in their put-down of possessions and the people who "hoard" them. It's supposed to be a sign of superstition, a hang-up, a social disease, greedy, sick. People who have things are derided as "fetishists." Why would one have a record collection when all information is available online to be had by the technologically plugged in (which is, at this point, a requirement for everyone)?

Why would one have a bookshelf when Google has taken all the book content in the world to be dispersed through its beneficent magnanimity? Books are heavy, dirty, dusty, and disintegrate into your lungs. Why should there be encyclopedias when there is the wiki-world? And so on. Why should there be record stores, bookstores, video stores, shopping areas, kiosks, cinemas, theaters, opera houses, libraries, schools, parks, government buildings, meeting halls, et al? Public spaces, markets, and interacting with other people are primeval, germy, and dangerous. After all, it can all be done online, you primates. The only thing one needs is a Whole Foods, some hip bars, and an airport so as to jet to Burma before it gets lame.

This is fine for the cyberelite; they can live as they wish. But why is their ideology impressed on all of us through this shame-based propaganda? Why is the "hoarder" so loathed by the Apple authorities?

Answer: because he or she is feared.

The "hoarder" has "things" after all, items like books and records which are clues to a past when these things were stores of knowledge, signifiers, totems of meaning. The cyberlords want it all destroyed. The library must be cleaned of nasty old books and filled with computers. The record collector must renounce his or her albums and replace them with an iPod. This is an obvious concern if the multibillion-dollar iTunes Inc. is to effectively rein in recalcitrant stragglers in a market it dominates so entirely, selling "songs"—which are, for them, just puffs of free digital smeg-phemera—for ninety-nine cents a pop. No resistance to the realm can be tolerated.

But it's not only the money they make from iTunes or their various other virtual marketplaces—which have left all physical businesses shuttered (aside from fro-yo places, nail salons, and gin-joints)—that they care about. The computer lords want to control everything, and central to controlling all things is controlling perception. Perception of the way things are, the way things work, and what's happened in history so that they can frame their version of events and control the narrative; mind-controlling the masses to make them into better, more compliant consumer/servants.

Just as governments spend enormous sums of money on textbooks, monuments, films, and museums which heroize their regime and frame their particular version of history, the computer overlords are concerned about the myths of the culture. Their ascendancy must seem inevitable, brilliant, brave, noble, just, and right.

The "stuff" that the "hoarder" retains, however, might tell a story which refutes or challenges their version of events in some way. The record collection or magazine or newspaper might reveal some clue to a social movement or trend or fashion or sensibility which defies their moronic stranglehold on consciousness. A burp of resistance. A clue to a way out. A signal that life doesn't actually depend on high-speed Internet access. And the physicality of the item infers that things meant something once, that everything wasn't always a meaningless, equivocal post on Tumblr.

Of course, the "hoarders" who are profiled on the show are extreme examples of people who hold on to things, but the message is nonetheless clear. Just as Willie Horton was exploited for racist ends and invoked to create fear and distrust of an entire group, the "hoarders" who are ridiculed, shamed, and "saved" on the television are meant to tar all owners of stuff with their brush.

The shaming of targeted "hoarders" is intended specifically to cajole, bully, and embarrass the population into giving up everything they have—not just possessions but ideas, ethics, rights to ownership (both intellectual and otherwise), privacy, decency, justice, fair treatment, and human rights.

In the Apple Internet age we are expected to surrender absolutely everything; anything less is filthy and deranged "hoarding." All content is free for the Internet lords who dispense it—or not—at their pleasure.

Apple Inc. is often seen to be selling an image or signifier of a lifestyle, but for them Apple is not just the means to life, but reality itself. Apple demands that everyone throw out all their other possessions for their ersatz mid-century plastic designs. These devices, which never stop "upgrading" and are therefore almost immediately obsolete, present a world where there is only Apple through which we get our information, our culture, our relationships, our sense of self, our love. Apple is the big apple—the world, the cosmos, sin, and godliness—and you've got to have it every day.

Apple's proposal would be impossible without the coordination of its dear ally, the Swedish megacorporation Ikea. Ikea, the original "i"-demon, is their ideological compatriot, and both are similarly ubiquitous features of the modern world. No dorm room or young person's house is free of middlebrow minimalist Ikea things on which to place their iPod, iPad, iPhone, etc. "iKea" manufactures items which paradoxically comply with the iWorld's "antistuff" doctrine: instantaneous furniture and utensils, created by slaves, that disintegrate or explode when moved.

II. IKEA'S CONSPIRACY TO SMASH ROMANCE

Ikea furniture is necessary for the success of Apple's antistuff doctrine. Not only because Ikea furniture eschews the future (its nihilistic furniture is designed for bivouac living), but because of its nefarious effects on domestic life.

When one conspires with one's partner to construct a piece of Ikea furniture, it is a harrowing task and speaks volumes of the faith one has in one's relationship. No matter that faith, it will most likely destroy the love affair or at least irreparably damage it, sowing the seeds for its imminent destruction. The instructions, supposed to be universal and written in pictograms, are embedded with tiny details, extremely easy to miss, that are absolutely vital to the success of the project. Wrong assembly results in nightmarish frustration, squabbling, and despair. The instructional manual always warns of impending death as well, casting a fearful morbid pall over the (ideally) mundane job of shelf building.

Why does Ikea make their manuals into time bombs of discord? Because Ikea wants couples to break up. Each breakup results in more bachelors and bachelorettes, which results in more Ikea products sold. Abandoned love affairs result not only in abandoned dreams but abandoned furniture, abandoned apartments, abandoned housewares, abandoned throw pillows and end tables left in the rain on the road or given away as Craigslist clutter.

Breakups are attractive to the Apple-iKea alliance for the isolation they ensure. An isolated population is more easily manipulated, misled, shorn of its possessions, its self-respect, and its sense. Romantic dissolution is the ultimate example of the imperialist's tried-and-true "divide and conquer" strategy. These corporations want the desolation of love: a population alone, miserable, confused, and in a state of self-loathing sexual desperation.

Both Apple and Ikea are closely linked to the pornography industry, aesthetically, philosophically, and economically. While home computers' popularity and ubiquity stemmed from their use as cryptoporn proliferators, both Ikea and Apple's designs stem from the ideology which spawned modern-day "adult" programming: Nordic functionalism. Indeed, the ideas of Nordic functionalism—a design idea which eliminated the buttresses, gilding, and facades of old architecture in preference for clean lines and modernity—resulted in the modern pornographic paradigm. Though functionalism began as a version of Le Corbusier and Bauhaus architecture, it ended as a total weltanschauung.

Along with the frills and indulgences of old-time design, this doctrine of socialistic simplicity swept away the clutter of the old world's baroque and courtly sex play and distilled it into the highly efficient erotica that is now standard fare. From its late-sixties beginnings (when Denmark led the world in decriminalizing smut), Norse pornography has been, like a science expo, brightly lit and clinical. An exposition of dispassionate technique and disregard for feelings, touch, communication, and affection. Form furiously follows function. Porn action, instead of being a lascivious sleaze-fest (replete with contrived story arcs) as it was in the "blue" era of "smoker" flicks, began to resemble lab work with moans and groans inserted like test data; pellets fed to rats.

What was the purpose of bringing sex into the light? Scandinavian design was an art of transparency. No obfuscation or sentimentality. Proscience and antireligious. Absorbing this philosophy, Danish and Swedish pornographers spearheaded the well-lit, unsentimental nudes which appeared later in hardcore "triple-X" features, ridding the world of the sentiment, treacle, and pretense of the Pompeo Posar/Bunny Yeager "cheesecake" era. The "girl next door" was duly evicted and her place rented by brusque sex workers in an assembly-line brothel. Ikea shelves are storage's unsentimental analogue. Frank, dispassionate shelves concerned with getting the job done, eyes glued to the bottom line. Beds are futons, a type of mattress originally used in Japan by prostitutes. Finnish cloth by Marimekko eschews plaids or complex patterns for simple, uncomplicated Rorschach blobs so one's living room becomes a psychiatrist couch of lurid—yet frank and clinical—revelations. Swedish and Danish furniture looks like the gear from a low-budget film production: director's chairs, boom lights, and simple pallets.

Facebook—and other devices for social control, neighbor spying, and mass surveillance—get their great power and ubiquity from the promise and lure of sex. Easy sex for free from multiple partners is the inferred reward. If people are coupled, in domestic bliss, this is less easily manipulated. Ikea wants to keep the population in a state of romantic flux. This is the reason for the hawking of sexual freedom, caprice, and whimsy as a bedrock of liberal civilization, as opposed to old control models which relied on sexual repression.

Ikea is ultimately a junior partner of the ascendant Apple megapower, which wants to erase history, strip people of all their belongings, and rehabilitate total poverty and cosmic displacement as modern, sleek, and fun. All this for complete control and ownership of the entire globe. Ikea has accepted the lieutenant's role in this unholy alliance. Like Apple, Ikea sneers at planning, permanence, and real possessions, beyond their ephemeral bric-a-brac. They suggest that the dorm room or living room or bedroom is just a momentary resting stop before we all become ultraefficient digital matter, buzzing at, around, and within each other in an eternal orgiastic cyber-cum-athon. But always orbiting the Apple deity: life-giver, death-merchant, illusionist; that from which all else originates.

How long before we're convinced that hands, arms, legs, and appendages are just bothersome? The cyberlords have already convinced us that maps, paper, pens, and even push buttons are somehow incredibly inconvenient and clumsy, leaving us scraping and pawing like drooling bug life on their flat and sleek digital dildos. Google's search engines, maps, etc., have likewise taught us to refrain from using our apparently out-of-date and hopelessly inefficient brains. What's next? Giving up all thought, consciousness, history, and agency? It's all just in the way.

"Hoarders" are the only thing standing between these incomprehensibly rich, all-controlling, degenerate, digital despots and the absolute destruction of any deviant or alternative consciousness—and indeed any nonofficial history or interpretation of the world. We must therefore say: *ALL POWER TO THE PACK RATS!!*

Help a "hoarder" consolidate and safe-keep their things today. Lend them money to rent a storage locker. Volunteer to help them keep their things at your place. Their stuff is the final shred of resistance to the destruction of all non-Apple-approved human endeavors.

4

THE RISE AND FALL OF COLLEGE ROCK

NPR, INDIE, AND THE GENTRIFICATION OF PUNK

OF ALL THE TYPES OF ROCK MUSIC, perhaps the one that is least considered and most overlooked is "college rock." Like today's "indie rock," it was named for the circumstance of its proliferation, rather than some characteristic or aesthetic of the music (such as heavy metal, noise, punk, grind, et al). Anthemic and clever, college rock produced clean pop songs which still resonate with listeners today. But what was college rock exactly and why did it disappear? And why is there no cult of stalwarts who maintain its legacy, as there is with nearly every other subcult of rock 'n' roll (goth, ska, mod, punk, rockabilly, etc.)? There is, for example, no Robert Gordon (seventies rockabilly revivalist) or Paul Weller (the second-wave "modfather") figure of college rock rallying a "college-rock revival"; at least not on the near horizon.

Though usually associated with groups of the early 1980s, college rock existed for a short time before and afterward as well, through the heyday of college radio. The genre's groups, though often signed to major labels, did not typically enjoy mainstream popularity but were instead cult favorites—a musical counterpart to the then-popular "midnight movie" craze where gonzo flops and campy outrages were displayed to a knowing, fun-loving, and unpretentious audience. (Of course, some of the college rock groups—such as Talking Heads, Violent Femmes, and REM—eventually became very successful.)

The genre wasn't called "college rock" because it was produced exclusively for or by students but was instead named for the radio stations which were its champion and proponent. In the sixties, when FM radio was less typical, the FCC issued many Class D radio licenses to universities, which allowed them to create noncommercial stations on the little-used left side of dial (typically 88.1–90.5 FM). Despite residing in the hinterlands, many of their signals were powerful, with tens of thousands of kilowatts.

By the late seventies, FM had become paradigmatic, and the college stations were burgeoning and sometimes influential. As opposed to commercial stations, which were committed to a highly restrictive "Top 40" format, college radio was fairly free-form in its programming. College stations saw promulgation of lesser-heard groups as their responsibility; their sacred mission. They were staffed by music enthusiasts who worked without pay, and who saw college rock as a desperately needed alternative to the platinum tedium of "classic" and Top 40 drivel.

While university students certainly comprised some of the audience of college rock, all kinds of people were potential listeners. Still, because of its ivory-tower associations, a certain type of education and class background were assumed of both the producers and consumers of college rock. If Lou Reed and Iggy Pop are the "godfathers of punk," Roger McGuinn and Jonathan Richman could arguably be considered the alpha college rockers.

College rock often had a vaguely political or satirical bent. After the campus takeovers of the sixties and seventies, universities in the 1980s were still considered progressive institutions, places where social consciousness and political activism could be found alongside toga parties and keg-stands. Universities had deftly weathered the culture wars of the sixties by pretending to be outside of commerce—benevolent institutions created as places for pot smokers to congregate and talk trash. By the eighties, *St. Elmo's Fire, Animal House,* and the Reagan-era frat revival were incinerating all traces of campus radicalism, but there were still a few lingering totems of the student power movement; one was college radio. College rock could therefore be seen as a last gasp of the revolutionary student movement of the sixties.

College rock could be defined as a middle-class and art-conscious permutation of radio rock, without the Year Zero pretensions of punk. Though just a scant decade earlier rock 'n' roll or "rock" had been vaunted as the vanguard of a new revolutionary consciousness, by the seventies it had become codified, established, and even conservative; particularly since its courtship of the country music audience with its "Southern rock" gambit (which begat Lynyrd Skynyrd, Allman Brothers, America, Molly Hatchet, Crazy Horse, et al). At the other end of the spectrum from rock's Southern affectation was rock's punk mode, which—though initially entertaining—had become alienating, remote, militant, and noxious (-looking and -sounding). A college rock variant was therefore necessary for casual middle-class rock fans, left cold by heavy metal, punk rock, Southern rock, and the breezy West Coast sound of Steve Miller Band, Fleetwood Mac, and the Eagles.

As previously mentioned, college rock's musical characteristics are not necessarily apparent to the listener. While it had some of the same bourgeois sensibilities as modern "indie" rock, it lacked the willful obscurantism. Indie rock is marked by "slacker" cynicism, aloofness, introversion, and formalism, whereas college rock was still goofy, political, risible, idiotic. There was hope and playfulness in college rock. It was still rooted in the ambition of making a "hit": popular music for radio play. College rock had to be fun; frat rock (i.e., Swingin' Medallions, Kingsmen, John Fred & His Playboy Band) and soul revues had long been mainstays of campus life, so college rockers were under pressure to entertain in a visceral way. Therefore, there was often a novelty, populist component to college rock that is missing in today's opaque, elusive, and willfully obscure "indie" world.

Many college radio stations had powerful bandwidth and far-reaching influence. These stations published their own nationally syndicated newsletter (*College Music Journal* or *CMJ*) about college rock trends and happenings. As a result, college rock's production values (with regard to discernibility, high fidelity, etc.) were configured for perceived "mass" tastes. Still, it was distinct from normal rock in that it was elitist, artier, and pandered to the Anglophilia of its middle-class audience. While college rock was informed by punk, new wave, and other subterranean trends, it was more "M.O.R.," with a roots element that would have been eschewed by those more radical elements, intent as they were on artifice, newness, aesthetic orthodoxy, and the destruction of tradition. Popular college rock bands included Violent Femmes, Guadalcanal Diary, REM, Love & Rockets, Robyn Hitchcock, Feelies, Shriekback, Fleshtones, Rank and File, Replacements, Hoodoo Gurus, Pixies, Elvis Costello, Haircut 100, Throwing Muses, XTC, the Church, Connells, and Let's Active. Most groups from Britain or Australia were given sanctuary at the left of the dial as its campus programmers would read the Anglo accent as cultured or educated; "one of us."

Simultaneous to the college rock phenomenon, the "yuppie" archetype of monied liberal connoisseur had been developed—a foil to lingering postsixties leftist boomers. The yuppie was an adult version of the privileged campus longhair who had outgrown the juvenile provocations and naive politics of his youth and now had a "pragmatic" approach to changing the world. This mostly consisted of buying things that were sensible, bourgeois, and decorous, such as Volvo station wagons and imported Italian olive oil. Their coed activist impulse was channeled in adulthood into improving their "quality of life," using material things which reflected their values: quality, wholesomeness, worldliness, and decency. French cheese, Scandinavian design, Italian espresso, olde-time American folk traditions, and many of the same sundries that would have been admired by the folk and protest movements centered around sixties college campuses.

The yuppie lifestyle was itself a cousin to the "Back to the Land" movement of the hippies; a protest against the grotesque mechanization of fast-food culture and the pervasive plastic crap of postwar America. But while the hippies' attempt had been revolutionary, the yuppies' concerns were merely aesthetic.

Central to the yuppie ideology was mature pragmatism; activism, communes, and protest weren't pragmatic and carried few palpable dividends. Making lots of money, though, was considered very pragmatic. Political opinions were measured. Shrill voices were a sign of imbalance. Privilege was to be enjoyed, though not too ostentatiously; this was in poor taste. Yuppiedom was heavily rooted in the Protestant aesthetic of moderation and decorum. Liking a sports team was a stand-in for community outreach; wearing a proletarian-style ball cap with the logo of a favorite team showed solidarity with the less fortunate better than any donation ever could.

As yuppie tenets became codified during the eighties, its adherents needed a mouthpiece through which to promulgate their values, spread their seed, communicate to one another, and also define themselves. This would be vital for them if they were to develop their ideologies, as well as to grow and flourish as a people. NPR, a public radio project of LBJ's Great Society legislation, was chosen as their party organ. Instead of becoming a target and whipping boy for "small government" privatization proponents (as the libraries, public schools, US post office, Amtrak, and NEA famously did), NPR grew muscle through generous donations by well-heeled corporate sponsors (Joan Kroc of McDonald's donated $250 million, for example) and set to work colonizing station after station at the end of the dial—right where the college stations traditionally hovered.

Claiming they were a detriment to broadcasting, NPR lobbied aggressively to destroy these small-fry noncommercial competitors, who were often forced to disband or convert to closed-circuit (campus-only) format. By the early nineties, college radio was squeezed to pathetic micropower status. Bullied and pummeled by *All Things Considered,* it ceased to exist as a variant to mainstream radio rock. An entire class of groups was disenfranchised, cut off from the casual listeners who wanted an "alternative" to the hair metal/R&B/classic rock triumvirate but who also weren't interested in the immersive, fanatic cults of American hardcore and postpunk.

The college rock groups died off. Into the breech leapt something called "indie rock."

"Indie" was a term borrowed from the English music papers and which initially meant "independent," as in "independent record label." The English music papers included "indie chart" Top 10s for groups like Felt and the Smiths to supplement the major label charts for people like Cher, Michael Jackson, and Bon Jovi. "Indie" was first adopted in America by Anglophilic, self-styled "pop" groups that arose out of the postpunk underground and who were influenced by these more obscure "independent" British groups. Indie fans, like yuppies, were extreme connoisseurs, seeking out groups to love that were so remote as to be essentially only rumored to exist. American indie groups took on the homemade aesthetics and subsistence economy of the US hardcore and postpunk bands—something not typical in the industry-driven UK music scene—and merged them with the yuppie's tastemaking and posthippie civic sensibility.

Stylistically, indie was usually "shambolic" guitar music which looked for the same amateurish spontaneity as punk but omitted the punk rocker's expressions of anger and their commitment to being unloved. Indie groups abandoned the possibly embarrassing politicking, kept some noise, and replaced the rough-and-tumble clobber with respectable jumpers and cardigans. Though they were in part a refutation of hardcore and punk, indie rockers were united to their black-clad cousins through economy; all of them used the same small clubs, record plants, copy shops, record stores, distributors, etc.

Chosen signifiers were subtle indicators that the

group in question admired a certain class of British ne'er-do-well bands. Sixties revivalism of a certain type and a kind of sophisticate infantilism were the earmarks of early indie. Many of these groups would have been college rock, but without the college stations to play their music, populism in record cover design or in sonic production was no longer a concern. It was also less possible without cash flow; the record company budgets which could have sponsored the college rock group, with its capacity to produce a small market "hit," had disappeared. Therefore, when "college" switched to "indie," it became much more obscurantist, lo-fi, remote, and personal.

Punk had been, in part, a response to the boomers' smug boasts of former glory; the ex-hippies' reminiscences of sixties street fighting, narcotic bravado, and bohemian politics pervaded the culture. Punk rock one-upped these claims to radicalism by creating a psychotic, sci-fi-cartoon, cul-de-sac version of leftism. It challenged hippie hypocrisy with an all-or-nothing model of doomed absolutism. It was as immersive as a motorcycle gang or membership in the Mafia; part-time participants were derided as "poseurs," while any deviation from orthodoxy was a "sellout." The punks were hyperconscious of race and attempted to mimic the black experience by transforming themselves into a distinct caste which was reviled and discriminated against by squares. Such militancy was for a time successful in creating an economic and social ghetto which was nearly impenetrable to corporate infiltration and which only adventurous or deranged souls dared enter.

The punk's jackbooted existentialism hastened the former hippies toward their pragmatic yuppie endgame. With nowhere to go, the next generation—the "indie" bands—played their guitars sheepishly and dutifully. The hippies, of course, had come out of a time of unparalleled affluence and the punks had been committed to poverty. But the indie rocker, scared of recession, didn't feel as heroic as these forebears and inherited some of the yuppie's fearful "pragmatism." They were also horrified by the proletarian element of the hardcore punk cult, which sometimes attracted "rednecks" or army types, and was ritualistically violent.

Since the pretense of the yuppie was a slightly world-weary wisdom born of the fractious street battles of the sixties and seventies, home and family were central to their image. While the yuppie was a traveled Europhile who loved the paella of Valencia and the chocolate of Belgium, he or she also adored a certain brand of Americana. Folky comfort and conservatism pervaded the aesthetic. Real estate therefore became a pet project, particularly redoing what became known as the "homes" of economically abandoned postindustrial US cities, in an evangelical attempt at urban "revitalization." Besides money, a nostalgia for the America of their parents was at the heart of their project. This was a guilt-ridden attempt to mend fences with now-deceased families against whom they had once rebelled so vociferously, and for whom they now felt pathos, kinship, and class allegiance. Posthumously, the yuppies celebrated their once-reviled elders as the "Greatest

Generation" and moved to reinstitutionalize an imagined version of their world.

As the yuppies took on a long-term project to "gentrify" American cities and remake them in their own image, the indie groups, typically the scions of NPR listeners (affluent, decorous, white), took on the mission to "gentrify" punk. With indie, the independent record label—instead of being an emotionally driven, "punk" rebel gesture against major label conglomerates who were considered clueless, exploitive, and evil—became a kind of "do-it-yourself" hobby similar to the restoration projects featured on yuppie fave TV program *This Old House.* As an indie label grew from hobby to business, it would self-consciously mirror major label tactics and business practices, but infuse them with the homeyness and wholesomeness of Martha Stewart's cooking and crafts.

Just as the yuppie colonizers took the rough, downtrodden, dangerous, sometimes nihilistic city neighborhoods which—though crushed by neglect—often housed vibrant communities, and "flipped" them for big bucks by making them palatable to middle-class normals, so did indie entrepreneurs take American punk and hardcore—similarly rough, tawdry, and ignored and reviled by capital—with its highly effective framework of distributors, fanzines, concert promoters, and community, and remake it into something which could be sold to mainstream rock fans of a certain class; the very people who had been abandoned when college rock collapsed. The term for this personal, individualist, capitalist, apolitical, entrepreneurial version of punk was "DIY" ("do-it-yourself"). DIY segued neatly with the by-now-paradigmatic yuppie creed and its emphasis on local, quaint, and home-made products. Underground shows, like the "revitalized" neighborhoods of the inner city, were cleansed of their wildness and strangeness, along with their skinheads and endemic bouts of violence.

The absolute success of these two movements is such that at this stage, "indie" and "yuppie" are meaningless designators. The yuppie aesthetic of connoisseurship has infiltrated everywhere and now there is only—for many of us—either luxury gelato or food made of chemical waste. Ikea, Martha Stewart, and Whole Foods make yuppiedom no longer a chic and extravagant choice but an enforced mode. It's either that or eat at a toxic toilet such as McDonald's. The indie aesthetic is likewise de rigueur. H&M, Urban Outfitters, and American Apparel sell the floppy "Brit on a holiday" look to all Americans. Radiohead and Arcade Fire music is blasted from speakers at stadiums. For many poor souls, there is no alternative to the alternative.

5

THE LEGACY MACHINE

THE ROCK 'N' ROLLER'S LEGACY is paramount; of thousands of groups with quantifiable careers, only a few are remembered. The rest—even if they played to wild applause at sold-out music halls during their heyday—are condemned to obscurity. This is a concern for the group, as historical remembrance is vital to the viability of future projects and continued back-catalog sales.

Groups are therefore obsessed not only with immortalizing themselves and their achievements, but in framing these things in a manner which will play well to future sensibilities. A legacy, however, is hard to establish, and one can no longer rely on fans—who are simply overwhelmed—to conjure it up. Indeed, more and more the groups have to rely on a general public of "nonfans" for validation.

Thus the modern phenomena of DIY self-historicization through film. Punk groups in particular have created a genre of rock documentaries desperate to explain their cult to modern-day Netflix viewers, people typically unconcerned with rock 'n' roll in the first place.

These films are a formulaic jumble consisting of: a) celebrities testifying on behalf of the group, b) grainy black-and-white photo montages, and c) music blasted as dramatic punctuation. At best they are agitprop, at worst the sort of mind-control brain poison manufactured by Madison Avenue. All are designed to convince the ignorant bystander of the group's specialness and singularity.

This concession to populism is remarkable for the fact that punk was designed to be an esoteric subculture, inscrutable to the uninitiated. A select group; a sacred order at an oblong table. But either for money, glory, or fear of being buried by history, its participants present it shorthand to hordes of anonymous couch potatoes in a quest for validation.

Such servility to the masses on the part of the groups and their biographers amounts to a grand betrayal. A den of safecrackers turned into snitches. How did this happen?

I. THE FANS

The modern rock model is a world apart from the classic scenes of teenyboppers screaming in orgiastic abandon for their idols. Instead of fans poring over album jackets and news items for clues to their favorite star's inner life, groups nowadays are greeted with nonchalance. Some ethereal frenzy can be had by brown-nosing journalists or paying publicists to "promote" one's group to some taw-

ernight
tadium
Tony
. . . conc
ough audien
d and the Be
concert for
. . at end of show
field behind the
nd sped off through
with four
waving from the windows . . . firs
er done that, according to oldtimers
the effects of the dis-
convention in Chicago.
WIDE WORLD
U. S. Space
OGO
servatories,
elliptical
satellite

dry website but, increasingly, no one seems to really care. Today's groups have to rely on themselves to construct their own myths. Self-veneration in lieu of fandom. *You must first love yourself before others will love you* is the logic possibly lurking behind the strategy.

Rock 'n' roll fans of the fifties, sixties, and seventies were a smitten lot—often preteen—who used their resources to buy scraps of a performer's hotel linen, start official fan clubs, draw pictures of their beloved musician, and write heartfelt letters to said star. This period of innocence, repressed hysteria, and religiosity toward the music was a feature of early rock 'n' roll, but it was part of a hermetic culture which couldn't long survive corporate America's "invasion" of the scene.

II. HOSTILE TAKEOVER

Though the early rock 'n' roll era has been historicized as a Mafia-run, payola-driven time of exploitation and corruption, record labels were often run by women, teenagers, and people of color; those who were entirely shut out of the corporate structure at the time.

Florence Greenberg (Wand, Scepter, Tiara, and Citation Records), Johnnie Mae Matthews (Northern, Reel, and Big Hit Records), Estelle Axton (Stax, Volt, and Satellite Records), Zelma "Zell" Sanders (J&S, Neptune, Zell, Sprout, Tuff, and Dice Records), Joanne Bratton (Golden World, Ric-Tic Records), Vivian Carter (Tollie, Abner, Interphon, and Vee-Jay Records), and Raynoma Singleton (Shrine Records) are just a few examples of women who were company bosses in the early rhythm and rock record game. Musicians such as Sam Cooke (SAR Records), Ray Harris (Hi Records), and Harvey Fuqua (Tri-Phi, Harvey Records) ran their own labels, while black men like Berry Gordy (Motown, VIP, Soul, Tamla, Gordy Records), George and Ernie Leaner (One-derful!, Mar-V-Lus, Toddlin' Town, M-Pac!), James Bracken (Abner, Tollie, Interphon, Vee-Jay), Ed Wingate (Ric-Tic, Wingate, Golden World Records), and Don Robey (Duke, Peacock, Sure-Shot, Back Beat Records) were among the period's premiere music moguls. This was the real era of "independent" records, when small, wildcat labels could—and often would—sell in the millions.

At the time, "major label" corporations like RCA, Columbia, and Capitol were often hapless bystanders to the business of teenage rock. They didn't know how to market it or identify it; they couldn't ingratiate themselves to the disc-jock tastemakers or comprehend the quick-changing language and styles. When RCA won world-shaking Elvis Presley's contract in 1956, they tried to transform him into a Crosby or Sinatra, and ended up snuffing his flame and nearly destroying his career. Indeed, the characterization of rock 'n' roll by the record "majors" as a criminal operation of payola and mafioso, in the years before their ascendancy put things aright, was partially sour grapes; their smear campaign of a renegade who was out of their control and running amok.

The corporations reined in the recalcitrants, however, when the Beatles took over in their whirlwind "invasion."

The Beatles initially appeared on black-owned independent Vee-Jay, but were quickly bought up by Capitol Records. After the Beatles, the floodgates opened for the rest of the Anglo groups, such as the Animals and Rolling Stones. This was a profound turnaround, in that it introduced a new argot to rock 'n' roll culture. With "British English" introduced as a dialect of rock, middle-class suburban Americans could now take their seat at a previously off-limits urban and hillbilly table. They were suddenly "authentic," simply by being American.

Exposing a repressed suburban audience to the implied violence of rock 'n' roll resulted in "Beatlemania," an orgy of frustration, desire, and lunacy. Media depictions of this feminine Dionysia account for the band-forming frenzy which quickly consumed Middle America; for the suburban male, building hot rods and playing football seemed suddenly passé. The "mania" was conjured out of the gobbledygook chants, harmonies, and incantations which comprised rock 'n' roll, with the "Fab Four" serving as the channel or conduit. But this kind of magic couldn't be sustained. All of the UK groups were tied to major labels; the so-called British Invasion was in fact the corporate conquest of a subculture, and the ensuing madness its death rattle—by 1968, independent labels were all but killed off or bought up by their deep-pocketed competitors. With the music corralled by multinationals, its audience lost access to the arcane, and this kind of mass possession hasn't been seen since.

III. MERGERS AND ACQUISITIONS

The corporate takeover of rock in the midsixties and the subsequent colonization of folk, jazz, and "soul" was a full-scale trauma to a fledgling industry which had initially been characterized by novelty hits performed by nobodies, as well as a democratization of participants, distribution, and production.

After the midsixties' corporatization and suburbanization of the form (1964's British Invasion), rock almost immediately co-opted and absorbed "folk music" (illustrated emphatically by Dylan's risky use of electricity at Newport in '65, the Byrds' "Mr. Tambourine Man," and Barry McGuire's "Eve of Destruction"), and with it, that huge scene's concerns about authenticity and capitalist collusion. With the folk merger, the rock audience also got, on average, a little older, more critical, and less willing to give themselves over to abandon, fandom, or carnal offering.

This changed the music dramatically. While folk's dissolution bolstered rock 'n' roll's numbers with a new monied collegiate constituency, rock 'n' roll (shortened to "rock" after its merger with folk) inherited many of the folkies' attitudes, leftover from their time in the coffee shops. An obsession with authenticity was one; that the music had to come from an authentic place such as the Delta, the Bayou, or some other rugged and destitute situation. Rock 'n' rollers, previously hollering about hot rods and cuts of clothes, were now required to sing the blues and adopt the rasp of a field hand. Another was contractual wariness; the idea of commercial or artistic "control." If one was too closely linked to the vulgarian record hustlers of the independent rock 'n' roll world, who encouraged their stars to hawk zit cream or lip-synch at record hops, one was a charlatan, a cheat, a liar, and low-class. Now, commercial respectability meant Protestantism; contracts with lawyers and proper show-biz management were part of a new bourgeois tool set used by the middle-class former folkies, replacing the old rock 'n' roll label paradigm of paying artists in cars and clothes.

Simultaneously, record companies divested from jazz as it went "free" and overtly black nationalist, leaving that music's audience bereft and searching. Therefore, rock's ranks swelled again, this time with a more academic, introverted, and urbane component, focused on "jazz" values theretofore irrelevant in assessing rock 'n' roll, such as virtuoso musicianship, seriousness, facial hair, and monkish dedication to craft.

Absorbing the jazz and folk audiences changed rock 'n' roll into something more diverse, with a constituency that was on average more self-conscious, academic, middle class, and worldly. The music which was marketed to this broad new audience reflected their varied interests; therefore a group like MC5 would play songs by James Brown, John Lee Hooker, Ted Taylor, the Troggs, Sun Ra, and Pharoah Sanders in the same set. The Doors would utilize beat poetry, and the Beatles would feature avant tape-collage, magick messages, and "world" music elements on their albums.

Rock's demeanor changed to something more systematic, irreligious, strategic, long-term, and dialectical, while the industry—instead of resembling the comic-book stand or illegal narcotics business it had before—began to imitate the rag trade or auto industry, with carefully honed PR messages and concept records, all of which fed into a new theme of "progress": that with each record, group, or trend, the music's quality was improving and becoming more "evolved." This "dialectic in art" idea was a hang-up of modernism, an aesthetic movement which had hovered around jazz for decades.

Soon, the jazz-inspired "progressive rock" ("prog") trend stated in no uncertain terms that the music was supposed to become something better, more important, heálthier, greater, via more virtuosic complications, conceptually themed records, and less fun. Records that would have been made in hours were constructed over months with lots of fuss and fanfare. This was quickly met with complaints, primarily in the forms of "glam" and "punk."

IV. PARADISE LOST

While the music lost its parochialism, a nostalgia immediately kicked in for "the garden," the early period when rock was raw, pure, and teenage, before worldliness set in and made everything a bummer. "Worldliness" in this case would be the rock-folk-jazz merger and ensuing concerns, such as reconciling the contradictions of art and commerce, how authentic or inauthentic various artists were, who the most virtuoso musician was, and what role art could have in the political transformation of the world. Most rock variations since this corporate crucible have been an attempt to recapture life in "the garden."

This wistfulness kicked in as early as Mothers of Inventions's postmodern *Cruising with Ruben & the Jets* (1968), the Beatles' postwop "Happiness Is a Warm Gun" (1968) and "Get Back" project (1969), the group Sha Na Na (1969), and even earlier with Joe Meek's productions "Tribute to Buddy Holly" (1961) and "Just Like Eddie" (a 1963 ode to recently deceased Eddie Cochran). Indeed, the remorseful cult to rock 'n' roll's lost innocence began almost as soon as the music was named and codified.

The "punk" mutation of the late seventies—which began as a reactionary refutation of folknik earnestness and jazzy "prog" noodling—was therefore an inevitability; it was only a question of what it would look like and what form it would take.

The seventies "glam" trend was a dry run which, being too one-dimensional and fifties nostalgic, didn't have the staying power of the more open-ended and sci-fi "punk" variant. While declaring itself a step backward toward greasy hair, flick-knives, and leather jackets (rock 'n' roll's golden "garden"), punk was actually a popular manifestation, and possibly the last gasp, of "modernism."

Modernism was the twentieth-century rebellion against the academy which started in the fine arts and crept into architecture, design, writing, and fashion. Central to modernism was the then-novel idea that art was political, a revolutionary tool. Modernist art movements were closely linked to communism, fascism, and other ideologies of the time, and proposed ways to transform the world through the art and items that people consumed in their everyday life. Inspired by World War I and Bolshevism, and reacting to the traumatic upheavals of industrialization, modernism challenged the academy, trashed technique, and declared the sky was the limit as to what could be accepted as art and design.

Punk—taking up the modernist's disdain for sacred cows, popular taste, and accepted ideas of success, legitimacy, and hierarchy—was a democratizing movement, its central tenet the insistence that "anyone can do it." This proposal, that art-making was for everyone, defrocked the anointed few who were regaling the world with pretentious bodies of work: groups like Pink Floyd, Emerson, Lake & Palmer, and Yes; all beneficiaries of tightly controlled national radio playlists, enormous publicity budgets, and a music history/scholarship designed to paint their contributions as genius, just, and right.

"Anyone can do it" led to a paucity of fans for every individual group. Instead of the audience members taking the role of wide-eyed enthusiasts, looking for a thrill, they became peers and competitors, which meant that each group would play to far fewer fans and sell far fewer records. This transformed not only the playing style of the groups, who affected an introversion and nonchalance which would have been anathema to an earlier era of entertainers, but also the economy of rock, as there was no longer a public to pay for the publicity, radio promotion, recording budget, movies, TV specials, stage sets, transportation, outfits, pins, and posters required for pop stardom.

Regardless of the new austerity, these conditions meant the group could create music without regard for the tastes of the mass—or "square"—audience which had been part of the equation ever since the corporate invasion/occupation. It was a utopian attempt to return to the "paradise lost" of early rock 'n' roll; the esoteric sensualism of the garden.

V. DIY

Following "anyone can do it" was the inevitable exhortation to "do it yourself." This was a cross-cultural seventies movement which had come out of, and outlived, the hippie era, and was typified by pamphlets and books like *Our Bodies, Ourselves,* a feminist handbook with tips on self-care. Shortly afterward, during the postpunk era (1978–1984), this movement was initialed, army style, to "DIY."

DIY was the byword through postpunk and on to the "indie" era. Now, with the economy destroyed by computers, DIY is no longer a philosophy as much as a requirement. Everyone is required to look after each aspect of their own art-making/proliferation because—ever since the Internet demonetized art, photos, film, writing, and music—there are few resources to support adjunct workers and technicians.

DIY now extends from the production of records, fanzines, and show promoting to all aspects of the rock experience, including fandom itself. Once, people venerated others. Now, under indie's DIY paradigm, people must venerate themselves. Historicization of the group is therefore now its own responsibility. Not only must the records and tours be DIY (arranged and administered by the bands themselves), but the hype itself—the historical biopics, the "remember when" nostalgia, the reunion demands, and the reissue records—is all self-generated.

Ironically, the Beatles—the biggest group of all, whose "invasion" unwittingly ushered in the corporate takeover of rock 'n' roll—started the DIY self-historicizing trend with their 1995 TV special *Anthology,* designed to hawk the group to an audience who had grown up without them.

The Beatles were, at the time of its making, three distinct and fractious individuals—as well as a deceased member who had been sainted in death after publicly disavowing the group and heaping scorn on their achievements for a full decade. Each Beatle's competing agendas and recollections are on display; the group members are perverse and contrarian, with the exception of Paul, whose pride of the group's songs, success, and what they meant to people is resolute and unflinching. George, on the other hand, nurses old resentments, Ringo is a slightly melancholic bon vivant with a cranky, sentimental view, and of course Yoko Ono, John Lennon's widow, is the anti-Beatle in many respects, who claimed not to know who the Beatles were or that the group even existed.

John Lennon, meanwhile, is a ghost who hasn't been

absorbed into a modern context or narrative. Lennon is stuck in time as a seventies self-help house-husband—isolated, manic-depressive, and revisionist—shrilly denouncing the crimes of the Fab Four. Throughout, Paul tries to put a brave face on the malaise of the other members. The group is collectively hungover from the trauma of Beatlemania and the toll it took on them, the expectations and alienation it engendered.

Their myth, with all these conflicts muddying what would seem like a straightforward tale of unprecedented popular success and innovation, will continue to thrive, not in spite of these conflicts but *because* of them. Other, more stable groups—such as the Rolling Stones, the Who, and Oasis—have contrived similar fractious interpersonal dynamics in order to give their own groups some Beatles-esque resonance, and thus generate more mystery, conjecture, and sales.

Punk and indie rock's DIY hagiographies, though, don't suffer the same internal contradictions and therefore feel more like the desperate advertisements they are. Typically not nuanced by democratic infighting, they are usually dull veneration, utilizing hapless stand-ins as directors to pretend that every shot and quote wasn't designated by the star of the film. These are often "crowdsourced"; paid for *by the fans themselves* before the abomination becomes public and makes money as a commercial item, propagating more revenue for the star-turned-"icon."

Such a status for their star is what these films strive for, as "icon" is essentially a brand, and a brand is something that's digestible to the fully detached, the otherwise oblivious; the reduction of the person to the slimmest, slightest object for the marginally engaged. This is self-objectification in the hunt for immortal status, like a poignant Greek myth wherein the hapless mortal, in a search for foreverness, reduces her or himself to a piece of plaster so as to have a place in the halls of Olympus.

For all of the punk rockers' stoic claims to independence, societal rejection, and aversion to fame, they really long to have their flesh rended by a Dionysian mob of shrieking Beatlemaniacs. The fearsome promise of these barely adolescent "maniacs," occupying hotels, breaking police barriers, and screaming nonstop for blood, constitutes a formative ur-text for the rocker, one which he or she can't shake. Its cosmic portrait of danger, magic, and *Lord of the Flies* anarchy figures centrally in the early programming of the group member, who wants, expects, and needs some version of it. Therefore, the modern DIY band—faced with the nonchalant peer-fan—looks outward to the masses for their own "maniac" mob, and takes what it can get.

VI. JUDGMENT DAY

The DIY legends, by bypassing the idea of a popularly determined firmament (i.e., chart hits, sales, pop success), have created a model where history is a series of explanations by people who claim to have been there or who apparently have special insight into what really occurred and what was important. Talking heads parade across the screen to explicate why a detached audience should care about some sordid group or scene of miscreants who never made it to the big time. History becomes a court, with witnesses on the stand who tell their version of events to a judge and jury. The jury is a passive audience of Netflix or DVD watchers who can partake of some wild underground bloodletting from the safety of their own bed and then lay claim to it, never needing to have taken off their bedroom slippers.

While this model can lead to lecture invitations, reunion tours, and digital record sales, it begs the question: why are members of the DIY or "punk" group, sworn in their lifetime to rejection of the masses, now prostrating themselves before the squares they used to despise, and begging their approval?

An audience who would never have stooped to check out the group or cared enough to explore "outside" bands or underground anything is now the validator of the group's worth, and a fully paid-up member of their club, despite never having been there. They are handed the scales of arbitration, despite lacking the experience or knowledge to judge the group, understand it contextually, or know whether the witnesses' accounts are trustworthy. Inevitably, the subject of the documentary will be declared "indispensable, seminal . . . a legend!!" and heaped accordingly with accolades.

This kind of hollow award, bestowed by normals who have no stake in the matter, is the sad outgrowth of DIY self-veneration; since there are no fans—only critics, cohorts, and competitors—the group must look to the absolutely disinterested for their support. To get this support, they must contrive a history that makes them fascinating to the channel-switching nonfan. This means the documentary must include celebrity endorsements, sensationalist hyperbole, and plenty of historical revisionism.

Such strategy ironically and tragically undercuts the DIY groups' original intention of creating something apart from "mainstream" culture and puts their legacy, their story, their secrets and esoterica, into the hands of an unwashed audience. While this audience didn't care for the group as a living thing, as roadkill they deign to hang it on their wall.

PART II

FACT-FINDING MISSION

DESTROY ALL FACTS

6

THE HISTORIC ROLE OF SUGAR IN EMPIRE BUILDING

IN THE MIDDLE AGES, when Europe first became aware of sugar, it was seen as a fearsome, possibly supernatural substance and was kept under lock and key, possibly the first of the "controlled substances." It had come north with the Arab conquest of the Middle East, North Africa, and Southern Europe, the "mad" stimulant which rode on the heels of the heretic. The Arabs proliferated sugar so avidly that it was said, "Where the Koran goes, sugar follows."

In modern times, the Muslim is characterized as austere, ascetic, and fun-hating, but for a millennium they were portrayed as profligate, sin-loving, licentious, and effete, with scented hookahs and rugs on the walls of their harems. Such was the projection of resentful, sweets-starved Christian Europeans onto the brokers and users of sugar.

In seven years the Iberian Peninsula fell to the Mohammedans. It took over seven hundred for the Christians to get it back. Why were the interlopers so intransigent? Why, in that era of fluid borders, great migrations, and topsy-turvy alliances, could Spain's Muslim rulers not be ousted?

It was because they had sugar on their side. Those who have befriended that stimulant have historically vanquished all foes. Sugar was difficult to cultivate, requiring advanced agricultural knowledge. The tediousness of the reconquest, so many centuries long, was possibly due to the Christian knights' latent fear of losing sugar once and for all. Just as prohibition was shakily enforced by backsliding teetotalers, the knights' fervor for their faith shrank in the face of the prospect of a confectionless world. Luxury is easy for the "have-nots" to condemn but difficult for the "haves" to relinquish. Perhaps the Christians feared that, in the heat of battle, they would "raze cane."

By the time the "reconquest" was finally realized, under the reign of Queen Isabella, sugar's cultivation had been mastered by Portuguese, Spaniards, and Azoreans, making the Muslims' expertise redundant and their presence obsolete. The final year of the reconquest, 1492, Columbus also made his historic voyage to the Americas on behalf of the Spanish crown. Since Portugal owned the plantations in the nearby islands where cane could grow, Columbus's primary mission was to establish a sugar foothold in faraway lands, which he of course managed, in spades. Indeed, for centuries the Americas and the Indies were first and foremost a massive slave plantation utilized

ates to
(on
efeller
kefeller,
acy on
run.
sion on
of the
regula-
ernight
Stadium
Tony
. . . conc
ough audienc
d and the Be
concert for
. . at end of show
field behind the
nd sped off through s
from the windows . . . firs
WIDE WORLD
he effects of the dis-
onvention in Chicago.
U. S. Spac
OGO
servatories,
elliptical
satellit
earth, and
give a

for the cultivation of confection. France famously traded "a few snowy acres"—a.k.a., French Canada and Louisiana—for some Caribbean islands where sugarcane would flourish. With exploitation of the "new world," the Arabs were outmatched as all classes of Europeans were inundated with the crystallized drug, previously only accessible to the upper elite. Afterward, the caliphate subsided steadily on the world stage until its eventual dismemberment by European imperialists at the end of World War I.

Imperial conquest in the new world was a race to create the most sugar. As much as oil or columbite-tantalite in the modern world, it was a diabolical commodity, the cultivation of which precipitated slavery, ecological devastation, and even genocide.

Not only because sugar was delicious, physically affecting, addictive, and profitable, but because whichever nation ran the sugar supply would rule the world.

What gave the sugar-sprinkled peoples of the world their historic advantage over their foes? Sweetened tea, coffee, chocolate, pastries, trifle, crumble, and cookies assured a workforce that was more amphetamined, more delusional, and had a greater ability to endure industrial privations. The sugar eater's dreams were bolder and more vivid, and as addicts, their complacency was assured via strategic control of the treacle substance. Indeed, sugar was a magic potion which manufactured, out of mere mortals, a superrace of psychotics, capable of stranger thoughts and grander ideas, who were less prone to moral hygiene, and more capable of utter brutality.

The Spanish and Portuguese were initially the rulers of the galaxy due to their sugar fields in Cuba, Brazil, Hispaniola, and Florida, though the French asserted a strong claim with sugar holdings in Guadeloupe, Martinique, and St. Lucia, as did the Dutch with their colony of Suriname. Like the Cold War of the twentieth century, the European colonists were involved in an arms race of ambrosia. The British ultimately prevailed in this contest, first with their invasion of Jamaica, then, after the abolition of slavery, with the possession of India, the historic birthplace of cultivated sugarcane.

With the Monroe Doctrine (1823), the United States announced that it too would enter the contest for the great sugar fields of the world, and the Spanish-American War (1898), which secured sugar-rich Cuba and Puerto Rico for the Yanquis, initiated the "American century" of US global preeminence. Conquest of Haiti, the Philippines, and Hawaii were the coup de grâce which made the USA the "sole sugar superpower."

But the first world's conquest of the less developed nations nagged at its conscience. Guilt of sugar consumption for the advantage it gave over the sugarless and for the insanity it had wrought on the pastoral preconfection world was rife. Attempts to rehabilitate the drug—and disguise the mass addiction to it—were many. Sugar became a ritual sacrament of a religious-spiritual sort, whether as a magical invocation of mythological or theological creatures (e.g., Santa Claus, the Easter Bunny) or as a reward for ingesting ho-hum food in the form of "dessert," the postcomestible high. Sugar, the unholy destroyer of worlds, was dressed up as a bunny rabbit, candy corn, bonbon, candy cane, and used as consecration for weddings or given cutesy, infantilized titles. Sugar, inextricably tied to conquest, magic, power, intoxication, and "play," became psychologically synonymous with sexual depredation.

Marilyn Monroe's character in *Some Like It Hot* is called "Sugar Kane"; with her pneumatic figure and breathy, bubbling pronouncements of promiscuity, she embodied her namesake, the legalized and even compulsory drug of choice for the masses. Her seduction of persons of great power and prestige (i.e., Arthur Miller, Joe DiMaggio, JFK, RFK) is an apt analogy for sugar's sway over the decision-making of the superelite.

The covert drugging of the world's population over the centuries is a powerful component in the illogical insanity of the systems which have taken root since its widespread introduction, such as capitalism, and its out of vogue, statist brother fascism.

When revolution occurred in Cuba—the primary source of sugar for the USA—there was a momentary panic in kitchens across the imperial world. When the "Bay of Pigs" invasion to regain the islands for US plantation owners was thwarted by Communists, the reality of a sugar-free America became something to consider; Kennedy might have been murdered for "losing Cuba" by a mob on a blood-sugar withdrawal freak-out.

When Johnson was inaugurated, he allayed such fears

by assuring the masses with a corn syrup substitute. The syrup from corn was actually even sweeter than sugarcane and absolutely plentiful in North America. Indeed, when the Pilgrims were starving, the indigenous tribes saved them by teaching them about "maize." Rather than let them die, the settlers were given corn, a slow death which would drive them mad over the centuries. It was the ultimate curse to bestow upon the callous invader.

The Johnson administration and the "Great Society" are remembered now as the high-water mark of American achievement, confidence, and general opportunity for society. Coincidently, 1966—midway through Johnson's term—was when real sugar use first went into precipitous decline, replaced by corn syrup. After the sugar drought, the empire went on its mad descent, marked by calamity, total corruption, general idiocy, an epidemic of political assassinations, and surrender to degeneracy.

The naked cruelty of the sugar years segued into the depression and flatulence of a corn-syruped nation, with disastrous results.

When corn syrup first overtook refined sugar in the American diet, it wasn't considered a suitable alternative. Social planners attempted to replace the nation's drug and fuel source—sugarcane—with other narcotics.

The "lifestyle revolution" promulgated by the midsixties drug culture—supposedly a grassroots rebellion—was a desperate attempt by social planners to replace the public's desperate hunger for the sugar high, which had been so sadistically stolen by the damned "barbudos" of Castro's Cuba. Anti-Fidel fever in the USA has always had a manic, even hysterical ring to it; America was a nation of bitter junkies, shrilly condemning their former dealer.

The Soviet Union's sugar deal with revolutionary Cuba was characterized as a subsidy for the island-nation but in actuality it propelled the USSR to its greatest peacetime achievements under Khrushchev, Brezhnev, and Andropov until the system was derailed by traitorous elements in the politburo who sold out the revolution to capitalists (1989–1991). This surrender of revolutionary ideals could be traced to the megalomania and above-the-law sensibility of the sugar-infused brain.

Meanwhile in the USA, the CIA fed the population LSD, cocaine, peyote, marijuana, pharmaceutical pills, crystal meth, belladonna, mandrake, ayahuasca, mushrooms, airplane glue, and gave the Mafia a free hand to sell heroin. Anything to placate the population, and compete with the sugar-rich economies. Drugs were ubiquitous in the postsugar years, promoted heavily in all media to both young children (e.g., *H.R. Pufnstuf*, "Puff the Magic Dragon") and adults (via Miles Davis, *Playboy* magazine, et al). A "health food" craze was also contrived, to persuade people that sugar-free diets were "cool." But illegal drugs, though effective as an antidote for sugar withdrawal, were problematic for mass assignation, since their role for government was more prescriptive (i.e., destroying radical groups and political movements, undermining class consciousness, etc.) and not intended for everyone. They were just a stopgap measure until a real solution could be found.

That solution was the development of a souped-up, distilled, and muscular version of corn syrup called HFCS, i.e., "high-fructose corn syrup." In 1977 HFCS went into heavy production as a sweetener and by 1984 had replaced refined sugar in Coca-Cola and Pepsi.

HFCS led to epidemic obesity, acne, and insanity (e.g., Pepsi drinkers Michael Jackson and Britney Spears), but on the surface it did the job. It sweetened at a much higher rate of efficiency than sugar ever had and induced a giddy, manic high in the user followed by severe withdrawal episodes marked by fatigue, depression, and nihilism. As abundant as sugar had been in its heyday, it had been too precious to put into everything, but with corn syrup's cheapness and ubiquity, this wasn't an issue.

High-fructose corn syrup was potent and plentiful and was soon added to everything, from bread and marinara sauce to beer, peanut butter, cereal, pretzels, chips, lunch meat, hamburgers, hot dogs, catsup, pickle relish, and mayonnaise, renamed as "Miracle Whip." Even after the dissolution of Soviet power and the end of the Confectionery Cold War, the USA shirked the sugar which had made it great. HFCS was a heavier narcotic and American palates were now inured to the old-fashioned flavor of cane sugar. For manufacturers, HFCS was so profitable that they lobbied for a continued embargo/political isolation of Cuba so as to effectively outlaw "the white lady." They feared a triumphant comeback of that barely remembered treat from the halcyon days of American expansion.

Still, warily, sugar started to reappear in outlaw kitchens and cupboards. Old-timers remembered the high it gave them, the illicit joys from their youth spent wandering the streets as addicts, hooked to the delightful residue of the cane plant. Mexican Cokes became highly sought after, vestiges of an underground connoisseurship, a badge of esoteric knowledge. Some chefs started producing food which utilized the arcane sweetener for a small, louche audience of culinary perverts. Whether these new sugar users can repeat the terrifying feats of their addict forebears remains to be seen.

7

TRUE ORIGINS OF THE INTERNET

I SEE IT STILL, IN MY SLEEP. Jimmy Wales's wistful countenance on the computer screen. He looks pained. His body isn't visible in the photograph, but we wonder, from his expression, if he isn't being subjected to torment or physical harm. He beseeches us pitiably for funds, donations, alms, and oblations so as to grow and nourish his noble monolith. Called "Wikipedia," it's a publicly built superencyclopedia. It is our obligation to bankroll it, he says; without Wikipedia we would just revert to our former status of cavemen, larvae, algae, and scum.

Millions have spent their adult lives laboring on his mastaba, ornamenting it, detailing it, constructing new additions, spin-offs, wings, and corridors. And they have created something unprecedented. Hailed as a wonder of the world, it has awakened the final shred of idealism in the globe's otherwise nihilistic inhabitants. However, the hyperbole was misleading: the Colossus of Rhodes, the Taj Mahal, and the Great Wall were all wonders certainly, but the "Wiki" is something else, something more profound. A grand monument to gnosis, it contains all of recent humanity's history, hearsay, whims, and wisdom in one handy Hypertext Transfer Protocol. Through its apparent vastness and democracy, it seems to redeem the entire modern electromagnetic mess.

Therefore, Wales is considered a kind of modern Napoleon. Like the rail barons, the empire builders, and the pharaohs of Egypt, he has successfully harnessed the masses to construct an edifice the scope of which boggles the mind. He's recruited an army of unpaid writers, researchers, editors, and scouts/spies/policemen who jealously officiate on each other. Now—on top of the sweat, knowledge, and guarded secrets of the herd—he wants their wealth.

And just as they drool to erect his superfetish, they give their money generously so as to bejewel it—to the tune of $16 million just last year. The pope, puttering through Vatican City in his pope-mobile, was surely impressed. Just who is this Jimmy Wales character and why does he have such a mesmeric effect over so many? The multitude had labored over Wikipedia just as they had slaved over the Great Pyramid—for free. And with no recalcitrant bitterness. They love it and trust it implicitly. And when he recently called them to civic action, against the looming SOPA and PIPA edicts, they sprang to life.

Such is the belief in the greatness of this entity that normally passive people, who couldn't give a toss about millions killed in Iraq, secret torture chambers, nuclear meltdown in Japan, or ecological devastation, were enraged and politically engaged when Wikipedia cued them to be, at proposed government regulation of pirated content on the Internet. When renegade congresspeople proposed laws (SOPA, the "Stop Online Piracy Act") in October 2011 to halt the unregulated pillaging of copyrighted information such as music, film, writing, photography, and TV via electromagnetic means, Wales bared his teeth. SOPA threatened the ideology of "freedom" as propagated by Silicon Valley potentates who—though they don't give their computers away for free—believe that all writing, photography, film, television, and music is everyone's right to own no matter what the circumstance or what the production cost. Wales and his coven were determined to stop these heretic lawmakers.

Wikipedia and its partner Google therefore invoked their monopoly on truth and information to rile the mob, who were rudely interrupted from watching a YouTube video of the Olsen twins eating pizza in slow motion. Wales & Co. declared a crusade, ordering their slave army, which numbers in the scores of millions, to attack those who threatened precious "online freedoms" with "censorship."

Wiki-Google also made symbolic protests, breaching their own empty rhetoric about "net neutrality." Google's pious "protest" against a congressional bill to combat Internet piracy took its shape as self-mutilation: they blotted out their (horribly designed) corporate logo. But Wikipedia, a greater paragon of net purity, not only closed it-

nilar to
Kennedy support
Maddox of Georgia, a conservative
his abortive candidacy on August 17
WIDE
inside
when the announcen
at Apple headquarter
tles were splitting up
Achtung

self down completely but also coordinated another seven thousand sites shuttering their webcams for the day. The action was a great success and public servants backed off of SOPA, chastised and embarrassed.

The public tantrum of these corporate bodies, when challenged on their desire for total control and wealth, served to shine a light on their ubiquity, influence, and insidiousness.

The harnessing of "people power" by billion-dollar megacorporations through viral grassroots campaigning was mass hypnosis reminiscent of Obama's run for office. Like Obama, the emperors of Silicon Valley are supposed to represent a new paradigm, distinct from their predecessors. But just as Obama is proven to be another run-of-the-mill imperial president, Wiki-Google, et al are not unlike old-style hucksters, porn merchants, plagiarists, bootleggers, counterfeiters, and advertising firms. Despite this, Wiki-Google and the other Internet czars have branded themselves effectively as something new and uncapitalistic. Like universities and hospitals (also businesses which pretend not to be businesses), they present themselves as noble, selfless, egalitarian, and democratic; part of mankind's pleasant if bumpy evolution into something less savage and more enlightened, like dolphins, Pleiadians, or will-o'-wisps.

The war against SOPA was cast as the Internet knight's victorious counterstrike against an encroaching totalitarian state, who won't let you watch *Mad Men* without a cable subscription. In their propaganda, the Wiki lords invoked not the reliable fascism of Nazi Germany which the government predictably trots out when marketing their wars against appointed bogeymen (Qaddafi, Hussein, Milosevic, etc.), but Stalinist authority: government as freedom-crushing busybodies who cut off the flow of information and ensure their populace a rigid, gray half-life in a gulag of privation and ignorance. Such was the American's imagined Soviet Bloc citizen—a tragically stunted cave-fish who was entirely desexualized due to an acute lack of *Superman* comic books and Chanel handbags. For the American, lack of commodities equals frigidity. Through the latter half of the twentieth century, Americans had been disallowed from learning any skill besides shopping and watching, so a life without such occupations seemed like a pointless, existential purgatory. Therefore, conjuring the image of Iron Curtain oppression and fearmongering about loss of free HBO were effective PR tactics for battling state control.

The Silicon lords' rise to power with their "worldwide web" had come in the immediate wake of the capitalist powers vanquishing the "evil empire of the East," so it seemed to the casual onlooker that the one precipitated the other. The dirt was still fresh on the grave of the Socialist experiment when, up in its place, sprouted an Ayn Randian supercharged adult Internet playground of total freedom and caprice. Replacing Commie exhortations that individualism be submerged for the good of the state were de rigueur personal computers and web pages which detailed the dull nuances of everyone's inner life. Replacing guard towers, esoteric doctrines of Marx and Lenin, and the shadowy secrets of the KGB was the complete disintegration of privacy, ideology, and thought itself in the new "Inter-world." The web world linked the people who had been "trapped" behind an Iron Curtain with affluent Westerners who purchased them through human-trafficking sites (i.e., *Russianbrides.com*). These were among the first features of the Internet which eventually evolved into similar social-networking sites such as Facebook, Tinder, MySpace, and OkCupid. The prophet Jimmy Wales initially worked in this field too, creating porn aggregator sites before his Wikipedia revelation.

The Silicon dark lords' invocation of Soviet-style despotism is intriguing due to the true roots of the web and the manner in which it resembles the most unsavory aspects of the Soviet era. If there's anything the antiprivacy, vulgar-transparency ideology of "connectedness" and rampant spying (via Facebook, Google, Carnivore, et al) of the Internet paradigm resembles, it would be Stalinist Russia. But this is natural, since the web's actual inception could possibly stem from top-secret Soviet work in parapsychology.

The modern personal computer and the Internet system being funded and developed by the military-industrial complex and conceptually driven by Randian "objectivists" is a story that is well known. But there are clues that it has even more nefarious origins than just development at the hands of the usual suspects (IBM, MIT, etc.).

In the 1960s, when the Americans were trouncing

their foes in the field of atomic missile development, the Soviets were advancing on another, extremely top-secret front. Called "psychotronics," the Soviets were intrigued by mind control via hypnosis, mass suggestion, telepathy, linguistic engineering, clairvoyance, and ESP. When US spies discovered the advanced nature of the Russian program, it sent the spooks at Langley into a panic. Mere muscle and might, after all—even if it was nuclear-powered dynamite—was no match for mind control, especially if it could creep across borders undetected and infect the populace with Marxist contamination. The DIA, NSA, CIA, et al, determined to close the "psychic warfare gap." The CIA clumsily struck out with their own debauched experiments: LSD, MKUltra, etc., but these, while deranging the antiwar movement, didn't succeed in crushing the populace under their yoke entirely; there was still diversity of opinion and a little nonconformity. TV and art were fine envoys of suggestion and social programming but they could only do so much. The CIA wanted to discover what the Soviets knew about pacifying populations, spying on their innermost thoughts, controlling the mass. With the USSR collapse, the Americans rushed into the gap, as the turncoat Gorbachev laid out the hitherto hidden goodies for the victors to see.

What did they find? No one knows except those who were privy on that fateful day. But whatever they were, the results of this collusion have been cataclysmic for the human race. Could it be a coincidence? The mind control techniques mastered by the KGB were undoubtedly utilized by the Silicon Valley crowd (already beholden to their Pentagon paymasters) and were used to instill total idiocy and complacency in the entire US population. What is the Internet but ESP, clairvoyance, astral travel, and linguistically engineered mind control for the masses? Called "the Internet," nothing—not the Inquisition or the death camps or Pol Pot's Cambodia—has come close to pacifying a population in the manner that its "worldwide web" does. And ironically, the most profound cog in the Internet's complacency machine is Jimmy Wales's Wikipedia.

For the first time since Nazi Germany, people have a single source for all answers, a direct valve which can satisfy their curiosity about why rainbows appear, what the radius of gyration is, and what make of automobile the Duke of Gloucester digs. And, through some arcane magick or unholy pact with Google, Wikipedia is designed to pop up first no matter what topic one types into whatever search engine. For the lazy journalist and the average schmo, it is simple, pure truth and is endlessly repeated as such.

Wiki also has a pseudoreligious aspect: it helps Internet users to give penance. For the droves of web addicts seeking to mortify their flesh after another sticky bout of D-listing, Perez Hilton, "12 Things to Do Before You're 25," "8 Reasons to Have a One-Night Stand," bath-salt hysteria, pressing "Like" buttons, or some other such nitwit distraction, Wikipedia is a Sunday-morning salve—for the lies, betrayals, and self-defeating debauchery which implicate each and every user of a computer, and for which we all feel shame, contempt, disgust, and chagrin.

But we must forgive ourselves for these transgressions. Can we blame the flesh for being what it is? Would we tease the shark with a tender child and then chastise it for taking a chomp? No. But we can blame the computer for what it does to us. Victims of assault are traumatized, stripped of basic innocence and trust. So are we by what the Internet flashes us with, molests us with, and compels us to seek out. In tried and tested Stockholm syndrome style, we want to redeem the groping, insinuating, addictive machine with a daily bout of Wikipedi-ing; polishing the grommet on the Wiki page of this or that wretched *Star Wars* character and grimly policing our fellow citizens who post "unverified" items.

The Wiki police force, like the East German Stasi, is anonymous, plainclothed, and ubiquitous. It is comprised of hundreds of thousands of ordinary-acting citizens who present themselves as something entirely different by day: bakers, builders, homemakers, engineers, you name it. But when alone in their computer room, with the screen eerily lighting up their face, they report uncertified interlopers on pet sites, and scour the realm for evidence of sabotage on whatever scurrilous and useless Wiki page. When the lord's lands are determined to be free of scoundrels, these robo-snitches lay claim to their own legacy through a perfectly crafted article about some infinitesimal subject.

Because the education system has been so degraded

since the end of the Cold War, with the complete surrender of humanism or any sort of hope for the future, schools are entirely subservient to "business," now considered the only honorable profession. Wikipedia makes this possible, because it excuses the population for its abject ignorance by replacing places of actual study with a fanciful "aether" campus. It champions laziness, lameness, immediate gratification, and lack of depth in understanding. It represents total trust in the monolith of the web, which is marketed as a benevolent miracle, not unlike asbestos was in the 1930s. Wiki repeats its own silly hype about Arab Spring as a Twitter revolution and Facebook's role in liberating humanity from its shackles, but the slant of the analysis is the same that we see from America's ideological mainstays, Bloomberg, AP, NYT, et al. The writers—Wiki slaves—all share an archideology of web as savior, life bringer, dragon slayer, etc.

All of them recognize a higher truth, a higher power, which is the Internet's liberating and redeeming goodness, with the prophet of that power being Jimmy Wales.

In 1999, the film *The Matrix* proposed a world in which the protagonists could plug themselves into data and be able to forgo the sweat and tears of reading, practice, homework, and discipline. The Wiki way of learning, with everyone plugged via their phone into all knowledge at all times, precludes any actual reading or analysis. The Wiki's ideology is a stand-in. Though Wikipedia is supposedly an unbiased, completely even source of information, the SOPA battle already revealed a virulent ideology, with teeth bared at the slightest sign of regulation by the elected pencil-pushers in Congress.

The SOPA bill was predictably struck down to shrill cries of glee from the i-mob, but at least it served to cross out one company logo for a twenty-four-hour period. For that, we can be thankful.

It upset the faithful that a wonderful, charitable public institution such as Wiki-Google was sad. Millions took to their Twitter, Facebook, and Tumblr accounts to register their fist-shaking indignation for the unhappy ogres. But the blotted-out logo should have brought us joy. The corporate signifier of a bunch of Ayn Rand cultists being invisible for even a day was a triumph for decency.

Why? Because Google is a huge corporation which draws much of its revenue from the free content on the Internet. In fact, computers as we know them are designed specifically to steal content from creators of content.

The bill in question is an upper-class spat between Hollywood and the tech industry, who know that without free porn, music, films, et al, two-thousand-dollar Internet devices (i.e., MacBooks) have a lot less consumer allure. With so many Internet sites shut down in protest, we were actually reminded that the "web" is just a phase; that it will be displaced just as VCRs, record players, and drive-in movies were. When the Internet is put into storage with the 8-track, things will be different. People might talk about stuff again, or go shopping at a store, or journey to someone's house to watch a film again. Who knows? No one can guess what form it will take, of course, but like

Christianity, Wiki-Google's days are numbered. It is up to us to make sure its time is short.

Like a new nation, Wikipedia inspires not only fanatic loyalty but also moral and civic dogmatism. Just as the US uses its "Peace Corps" to rehabilitate imperial depredation with a bushy-tailed front group who teach ancient cultures how to take a dump, Wikipedia gives the radioactive bacteria mound of the Internet a fresh coat of paint.

Wikipedia winks haughtily at those caught in the web's Medusa stare. It is the crown jewel atop the pile of crap on the mound of dung in the cesspit of the Internet.

As victims, we must identify our foe. And on identifying it, we must stand firm. If the Internet is the problem, it is the entire Internet which must be confronted and defeated. Including the "good cop" Wikipedia.

poli
PERSONALITY CRISIS
the summer came, no
put on shows here, so
was put together, an
gig with AUTOMATIC
and NEOS. By Septe
shit together, and pu
O.A.P. with our you
CRY, ELSA, CRY FOR LOST MARK MERLIN--! I MOURN FO HIM, TOO- FOR THE MEMORY HAVE OF FORMER BUT NOW NEW CHA IS HERE BATTL THE UNK

8

THE DOCUMENTARY CRISIS

OIL PAINTING HAS BEEN PURSUED for around six hundred years. Screen-printing was developed during the Song dynasty in tenth-century China, making it around one thousand years old. The oldest known poem is Gilgamesh, written in cuneiform in the third millennium BCE, making written poetry at least five thousand years old. Music probably emerged along with Homo sapiens in Africa as an intrinsic feature of human culture, 160,000 years ago. Cinema, till this point, has had the life span of an American box turtle: approximately 124 years. Although just a babe in "art years," it faces an existential crisis.

Despite being hailed by Lenin as "the most important art form" during its infancy, able to transfix the world until recent generations, film now struggles for life, for relevancy, for viewers, and even to resemble something worthy of discourse at all. Since it developed out of topsy-turvy industrial capitalism, this condition of crisis is not so strange. In fact, as capitalism's persona is perpetual crisis, it makes sense that film—a chip off the old block—would be marked by the same manufactured hysteria that typifies the system which spawned it.

When it first developed into something more than a novelty, film was primarily an extension of the theater: a way to tell stories about the world. Unlike theater, film was the industrial era's contribution to art, and therefore—as opposed to other, more ancient mediums—it inevitably resembled the new industries, such as steel and oil, with the same stratified division of labor: unions, strikes, insidious contracts, pitiless exploitation, and monopoly-minded owner elite.

Indeed, since ownership of the means of production is the central issue in such types of industry, the great film houses—Warner Bros, MGM, et al—contrived a stranglehold on film, film processing, supply, workers (actors and directors bought and held under contract), and distribution, so as to stifle, destroy, and otherwise discourage competitors.

Thus, like rock 'n' roll in its "classic" phase, film in the USA was, almost from the beginning, an unaffordable venture for all except the Hollywood studios, with a few designated "auteurs" holding forth with their new offerings each season. Humanity was hypnotized by the fables they were taught in the hermetically sealed movie houses that dotted every city block. To be a participant in "the movies" was a glorious dream. Would-be actresses hurled themselves toward the merciless megalith of Hollywood like so much sacrificial foodstuff. To be a director was a laughable, fanciful ambition, akin to being president or king of the world.

When video technology was proliferated on the cheap beginning in the 1980s, it was of course, like all new consumer gizmos, hailed as a revolution for the everyman. It was cheap, portable, and outside of the film industry's monopoly over the means of production. Now anyone who had the smarts and the ambition could make a film, regardless of special show-biz connections, family ties, or casting couches. Like most supposed triumphs for "the people," this was one industry (Japanese electronics) asserting itself over another (Hollywood movies).

The only problem with video was its crudity and ugliness. The picture was rough and it didn't have the same magical sensibility that viewers saw in celluloid. Therefore, despite the almost immediate mass proliferation of video cameras, few films of any note were produced using the new equipment. Instead, the now ubiquitous camcorders were carted dutifully to underground rock shows until another use—documenting sex acts—was discovered.

Hollywood responded to the threat of video democracy, though, by making their means of production even more unassailable. Films were driven by supercelebs and special effects more than ever before. Storytelling was a low priority next to monster makeup, interstellar explosions, and megastars. As cable television and rental video continued to smash away at the revenue of the cinema house, the desire to produce spectacle was the overriding concern of the studios. For a film to have a theatrical release, it had to resemble a carnival ride with the attendant thrills, chills, and nausea-inducing spills. Breakneck editing, zany camera work, excruciating volume, and lurid, freakish violence have now made many films ironically unwatchable. Every year or so, due to forgetfulness, one may wander into a theater, lured by a hysterical advertising barrage, convinced that seeing a particular film is indispensable to one's continued cultural literacy. Then, emerging sullied, degraded, insulted, and twenty dollars poorer, one swears never to be tricked again. This life lesson is typically learned about once a year. In fact, movie-watching in a theater is generally an exercise in nostalgia, based on hearing a Drifters song on an oldies station.

This decline has been long coming. Jean-Luc Godard notes in an interview that when he discovered cinema in the fifties it was in fact "already over." Indeed, in 1946 America, with a population of 141 million, 100 million film tickets were sold each week, for a total of 3.65 billion tickets that year. Now, with the US population more than double that, ticket sales for all of North America in 2014 (including Canada) were just 1.27 billion.

Of course, people are still passively watching their master's morality plays, but at home on television, so picture quality is no longer as important. Sensing an opportunity for breakthrough, video makers—people not necessarily anointed by the studios—started trying to exploit the enormous potential for a decentralized movie industry, comprised of real auteurs and enthusiasts, similar to decentralized scenes of musicians, painters, and poets. But the video camera's initial utilization as a recorder or documenter was never shaken. Nor was the universal disdain for something which could film just anybody or be afforded by anyone. In a society without class consciousness but with an institutionalized contempt for poor people, video's very cheapness was actually a liability.

Because of its roots in recording music shows and sex acts for pornography, video was seen as "truth." Therefore, the new generation of filmmakers, barred from the use of actual film by its increasingly untenable expense, bothered themselves with making "documentaries" with their video, instead of dramas. Documentaries are now produced at an unbelievable rate, typically portraits of an unusual person, such as an archer with no arms or a vegetarian who hunts, or a political diatribe about the war, or a historical piece celebrating a particular rock group featuring testimonials from people who were "there" or were profoundly affected. Grants for documentaries are comparatively easy to come by, and documentary festivals abound.

While a portion of these video documentaries are interesting, what is fascinating is the *volume* of them that are being produced, in comparison to traditional fictional narratives. What does it mean if a generation can't seem to write a story with characters or a plot with tension? While music has gone absolutely fantasist (rife with "psych-folk" singer-songwriters wailing about magic and elves, electro composers proposing sex with robots, and alt-country crooners lamenting the passing of an imaginary world), many new filmmakers are obsessed with presenting a picture of "reality." They have a doomsday cult's concern with presenting their time as they see it, since they are disbarred from the official surreal dialogue which is being inscribed by imperialist lechers like the *New York Times* and the *Washington Post*'s Bob Woodward.

While this impulse to present one's own era to the Earth's inheritors is a human need, echoed in the cave paintings of yore, the artlessness of the medium needs to be taken to task. These films are usually bad-looking, unnuanced, propagandistic tellings of events. The camera work is almost always execrable, the narration is simplistic, the method of storytelling is usually a parade of talking heads; they feel like audio-visual presentations in a grade school. While utilizing this powerful medium and trying to express a particular ideological argument could be admirable, the aesthetic decisions of the video auteurs often reveal an infantilized weltanschauung, a stunted artistic vision, and a linear and impoverished mindset.

It all calls into question: who is the imagined audience for such expositions? Is it one's contemporaries? This seems highly unlikely since the retelling of Iraq War tidbits or the rock 'n' roll mythos featured in such pictures are usually well known to their watchers. If the point is a mere recitation of folklore, that is a defensible raison d'être, though the trappings of cinema hardly seem necessary for such a task when a pamphlet or magazine article could do the job at least as well, without all the self-important fuss. Making money can't be the reason since these projects are typically a financial risk.

The obvious answer seems to be that videos are produced to explain ourselves and our situation to some future alien race.

The documentary's careful and childlike elucidation of events are calculated to be understood by an exotic sensibility, and their genial idiocy seems like careful consideration of an interstellar consciousness of which no subtlety can be presumed for fear of misinterpretation, and for whom no common culture can be assumed. Why else would a film like *Standard Operating Procedure* (2008) be so asinine and simpleminded? Everyone human who saw that particular film must have been baffled at its apologist stance for what everyone knows is an ethics-free killing machine, the United States Army.

The other apparently pointless documentaries are legion. *No End in Sight* (2007), for example, is a propaganda piece that suggests that the war in Iraq was "mishandled" and then raises the specter of Iran as bogeyman in its closing statements, leaving the door open for a spectacular sequel. With these views palpably omnipresent on television and in the papers, who are the intended viewers for such abominable drivel? Perhaps a future race who will sort through the detritus of our civilization and to whom the filmmakers feel a responsibility to in explaining their damnable capitalist ideology, the system which spelled an end to such a luscious planet. Perhaps they believe that while the transmissions of television will be lost, and newspapers burned away in the nuclear holocaust, the video documentary will survive, protected by its tough plastic DVD sheath. Their propaganda is supposed to mitigate the disgust the aliens feel at human senselessness, the same feeling you get when you find a great record collection at a thrift store that's been stepped on, scratched to hell, and left to molder.

The clues are all around that documentaries—and video in general—are meant for aliens. Why are DVDs shaped like flying saucers? To appeal to aliens. Why do pornographic actors shave their genitals? Because their directors imagine this will appeal to the aliens for whom the video porn is actually meant and who are commonly depicted as hairless. Who determined that video would be used this way? No one in particular. It was unconscious. Something about video screams "The Future" to people. Video fonts and screens always feature in futuristic television, records, and films. Perhaps there is some astral travel we've made through which we've witnessed this posthistorical environment.

This impulse—to create explanations of our time for a future superior race or being—is understandable of course, being the impetus for much esoteric and religious writings through the ages. But it's a mistake to assume that the aliens are so aesthetically stilted that they can't appreciate a little artistry in their propaganda. What the videos are really explaining to a future race is how stylistically impoverished our era has become. From the new buildings authored by a diabolical breed of "architects," to the office workers' khaki pants, to the artless business signs in the same few computer fonts, to the cars that are designed using the same horrible computer, the population is being aesthetically defecated on, and they know no better. Years of artistic retardation and philistine admonitions against art from everywhere—whether it's the Jesse Helms's of the federal government, or the rock 'n' roll stars of the culture industry ("A French Small Faces EP cover can piss all over any of [Picasso's] paintings," to quote Paul Weller)—have resulted in a kitsch country (the USA) that looks like shit and, through that country's outsize influence on the rest of the planet, a kitsch world that also looks like shit.

Of course, it's important not to be too harsh in one's judgment of the auteurs of these mediocre video movies. They are working under a fascist dictatorship, after all, with its attendant psychic torments, idiot population, and nasty bedfellows borne of the need for funding. It is especially difficult to produce anything worthwhile when one senses there is no audience for it. The mass media has successfully made us all feel remote, hapless, crazy, alone. Certainly, relatively little interesting art was probably produced in Pinochet's Chile.

Bob Dylan's famous interview in *Don't Look Back,* when he chastises a *Time* magazine reporter by saying, "There's no ideas in *Time* magazine . . . just these facts . . . Even the article on which you're doing, the way it's gonna come out, it can't be a good article . . . it means nothing . . ." he might as well have been discussing this new documentary craze. When, upon being pressed for an alternative approach, he suggests, "A plain picture . . . a plain picture of, let's say . . . a tramp vomiting, man, into the sewer . . . and next door to the picture, you know, is Mr. Rockefeller . . . on the subway going to work . . ." he could easily be talking about the collage newsreels of Santiago Álvarez.

Santiago Álvarez points the way toward the solution to the current quagmire the documentary film/video world finds itself in. A Cuban filmmaker who was charged by Fidel Castro with producing newsreels upon the revolution's successful bid for power, he created an average of a film every two weeks for thirty years. He did this with almost no materials at his disposal, and yet his constructions are fantastic evocations of the circumstances they were concocted in. An alien viewing his work would certainly be delighted at the humanity which created it, would understand the complexity of this breed and the circumstance and the contradictions in its characters which ultimately led to the destruction of the planet.

Sort of like if the aforementioned ruined record collection at the secondhand shop had a poignant explanation that elaborated the owner's struggle against the dire forces which created the calamity which ultimately befell it.

One of Santiago Álvarez's films worth watching is *LBJ*, made in 1969. It insinuates that LBJ was complicit in the assassinations that plagued the era (L for Luther, B for Bobby, J for Jack), and does so with almost no words or narration except found music. The tools are stark: A few *Life* and *Playboy* magazines, untorn and slowly panned across with the camera. Ingenious editing. Bewitching use of music. This is a documentary which could be played to any language group to similar effect and also works divorced of its political program, as beautiful collage art for the ages. The music—by Carl Orff, Miriam Makeba, Nina Simone, the Trashmen, Pablo Milanés, Leo Brouwer, and others—follows LBJ's daughter's marriage through to his dastardly deeds and closes with the birth of his grandchild, montaged with footage of war crimes perpetrated by the USA in Vietnam. Almost all of it is using pictures from the newspapers or the society pages of magazines. Álvarez is free to use whatever newsreel footage, magazine photographs, found images, and pop, jazz, or classical tunes as soundtrack he chooses, and from whatever sources he wants, since he is working for Instituto Cubano del Arte e Industria Cinematográficos of the Republic of Cuba, who were and still are in a state of war with the capitalist world, and therefore disdain copyright laws.

Envious filmmakers will watch Álvarez and cry, "No fair!" when they see what this allows him, but they should quit their bellyaching and get with the program. Modern licensing and intellectual property laws have destroyed art and expression in this country. It's time for the rebellion against filmic conventions and, yes, the laws that enforce modern film's mediocrity. Santiago Álvarez made over seven hundred films in his career which began with Fidel Castro's ascension in 1959 (when he was already forty!) and ended with his death in 1998. And Álvarez's work would be much better appreciated by any aliens who happen to wander by than the hokey simplistic garbage that the documentary makers are typically churning out nowadays.

9

THE ARTIST, ALIENATION, AND IMMORTALITY

I. ALIENATION

THE DEFINING CHARACTERISTIC of the rock 'n' roll group is not electrification of instruments or the colonization of outsider music. Nor is it a rebel pose, outrageous hairstyle, or daring footwear. The characteristic of the rock 'n' roll group which sets it apart from other art producers—the reason it is the most modern of all art producers—is that the group's stature has little relation to what it produces.

The group, after all, is not its records, its songs, or its concerts. The group hovers above what it produces; the group is just the group, and the promise of its particular proposal. People may love a group despite their terrible records, their boring concerts, their lack of charisma, etc. The group likewise treats its records coolly and its concerts as ephemera; none of them really *are* the group.

The group always maintains that it is better than the

things it does, which are the unfortunate products of particular circumstances. These are always either a case of an idiot producer, incompetent sound person, bad crowd, or a momentary lapse; "we were sick" / "I was drunk," et cetera.

Conversely, other artists' stature and identity are determined by the work that they produce. Matisse, Jane Austen, Godard, and Beethoven weren't beloved or renowned because of some ineffable quantity which was bestowed upon them. It was their oeuvre or "body of work" which, at least initially, heralded their notoriety. But the rock 'n' roll group is different; as opposed to other art makers, what the group "does" is separate from what the group "is."

This situation is ironic because, at a glance, a group appears to reconcile the alienation at the heart of the modern postindustrial malaise, whereby people are divorced from the fruit of their labor, the source of the things they consume, and their community and political process.

The group, briefly surveyed, seems to represent a successful defiance of such conditions by ensuring the participants a direct role in their destiny and the art which they produce. But a closer look reveals that the group, once named, takes on a life outside of its creations.

Indeed, rock stars from the beginning express ambivalence about the groups they construct, feeling outside of them, bullied by them, sick of them, imprisoned by them. Even when they slay the group-beast with a suicidal "breakup," it still guides them, haunts them, derides them from the grave, oftentimes gaining otherworldly power and stature in the afterlife.

The songwriter in the group quickly finds that no song or record can serve as a corrective to what the group is in the minds of its onlookers, and that he or she, a participant in the group, may have been a spectator—or the host-body to a parasite—all along.

Groups like Black Flag, the Runaways, the Grateful Dead, the Germs, P.I.L., Crass, the Shaggs, Slayer, Lynyrd Skynrd, Einstürzende Neubauten, Minor Threat, LiLiPUT, Ultramagnetic MCs, Wu-Tang Clan, Pussy Galore, Death in June, and Throbbing Gristle all reveal how groups live outside of their "output"; they are cults which define lifestyles and ideologies separate from whatever songs or shows they produced.

Black Flag's "bars" symbol signifies an ideology of perversity, toughness, cynicism, and black humor, and is tattooed on the necks of legions who have never heard the group. The Grateful Dead's "dancing bear" and "steal your face" logos represent a libertarian "gypsy" lifestyle; apolitical but antiauthoritarian, pleasure-seeking, grubby, and committed to outsiderism. The "Deadhead" usually doesn't listen to "The Dead." This doesn't detract from their authentic status as a Deadhead.

The group—even after its demise—is a speculative foundation, whose aesthetic *promise* might create scores of sycophants and true believers as opposed to its actual production output. A formerly insignificant group or performer can also be instilled with "legendary" status through manipulation of history or a well-timed discovery of their existence. This is convenient for the culture industry that wants to bend historical events, modes, and trends according to its needs.

The rock 'n' roll group/performer, whether it be Scritti Politti, Johnny Thunders, Nina Hagen, Gram Parsons, Elvis Presley, Bruce Springsteen, or countless others, owes much of its legend not to great recordings or fabled concerts, but to some other mystery; a cosmic designation which has as much to do with what they seemed to embody as to what they actually did.

This alienated aspect of the star—group—performer is what allows them to transcend time and space and achieve such resonance in disparate cultures and class groups. Because the group's power is tied only tangentially to their music or appearance, they float above changing styles and become a kind of specter or immortal being.

One often hears that the artist strives for a kind of *immortality.* Immortality is a quality which, in the popular imagination, is related to God, vampires, ghosts, and nuclear radiation. These things—besides being terrifying to humanity—are unified by the common condition of *total alienation.*

The vampire is alienated from humanity, who it must feast on to stay "alive." The ghost is alienated from its former physical body, and the rules that once governed it. God is alienated from His or Her subjects on Earth; while nuclear radiation—used by the Americans to bomb Japan, and then waved around for a half-century to ensure US

TIDE, JERK WARD (who you wouldn't believe), and the SANE. It turned out great, an omen for our future.
B.Y.O will be putting out a tape with local talent and pan-Canadian stuff. RED TIDE has a new tape out, as do JERK WARD. You can get both through Ken Jensen at 505 Ridley Dr, Victoria BC, Canada V9C 2A3. Soon to be out is the second DAY-GLOW ABORTIONS LP, a cassette from AUTOMATIC SHOCK, and possibly an LP from the NEOS.
Any bands wanting to play Victoria, please contact me, Jeff Helgason, c/o B.Y.O. Victoria, 3186 Metchosin Rd, Victoria B.C., Canada V9C 2A3. The phone # is (604)478-3145. Please get in touch at least month ahead of time, and give your date of birth and social security number for acquiring your work permits. Thanks, Jeff.

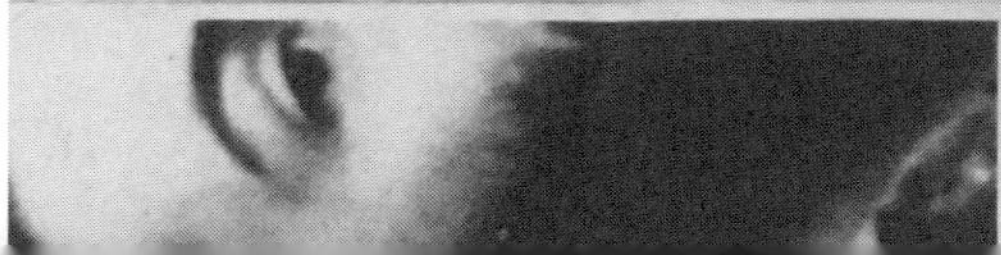

Dodge Charger kept aerody

DC
STRANG
ADVENTU
The RUNAWAY
THAT COMET IS CHANGING US ALL INTO STONE-AGE CAVEMEN!

The
seat

TY LOOK

many safety
mobile de-

supremacy over any who wouldn't submit—is the alienated weapon, wielded by a war machine that is terrified of utilizing it for its world-ending effects.

The modern artist is also an alienated being, at odds with society and normal ideas of work, time, morality, and comportment. In fact, the artist is synonymous with a state of alienation. Alienation is what gives them vision to dismantle and reveal the world. If an artist is not alienated, he or she is considered to be boring or a "sellout," and their work garbage.

How does the artist achieve such alienation? Why do they, like a ghoul, desire immortality? Is the artist a god, vampire, ghost, or piece of radiation?

II. ORIGINS OF THE ARTIST

Once, under Christianity, immortality belonged to everyone.

After one died, God could grant eternal life—or not. If God did not grant eternal life, one would burn in the Lake of Hell forever. Either way, immortality was achieved.

When the bourgeoisie took power in "the West," beginning in the seventeenth century, God was defrocked; reduced to second-class status beneath the brokers, bankers, realtors, developers, and financial speculators who were celebrated as lord-deities in the new money-religion paradigm called "capitalism."

The bourgeois coup was manifested in Great Britain with the English Civil War (1649), and by the Masonic revolutions in North America (1776) and France (1789).

Elsewhere, its ideology was spread with the movements of neoclassicism, liberalism, and the so-called scientific revolution. Such consolidations of bourgeois power were heralded by the Renaissance in the Netherlands and Italy and that movement's promulgation of the bourgeoisie's vanguard weapon, the artist.

Through these, the new capitalist class displaced the old titled royals and landed gentry, who withered away into irrelevance. This putsch was only achieved with vital assistance from the emerging "arts."

Just as the aristocracy had employed priests to explain their own divine right, the bourgeoisie invented their own magical imp, called "the artist," to explain and celebrate their own rise to power. It's not a coincidence that "artist" sounds very much like "atheist"; the artist was invented as a gladiator to kill the old god for his paymaster. After victory, the Kingdom of Heaven was, along with God, thrown in the dustbin.

To seize power, the bourgeoisie had required the demotion of the church and the clergy who had explained the divine right of the aristocracy. But in this necessary reduction of God and simultaneous celebration of science, they had closed the old avenue to eternal life, even to themselves.

Becoming a god on Earth therefore became the goal. This required total control of the population and the Earth's "resources"; appropriation of the deity's cosmic abilities as well as his wealth and domain. The sciences were unleashed to wreak whatever they could, regardless of ethics or implications. The transformation of the world through scientific discovery, technology, and development was accelerated at cataclysmic, traumatizing speed. The subsequent cosmology ensured the nascent capitalist class' grip on absolute power and also presented a version of the world wherein they were the central feature.

III. THE ARTIST AS GOD

Immortality became an obsession of the bourgeoisie, who hoped it could be attained through the artist's portrait. Later, they would use trusts, endowments, legacies, names on university buildings, health food, and cryogenics, but initially it was the painted portrait. This is the reason why, in depictions of rich burghers, their manors are lousy with oil paintings of their clan. Being imbued with the power to grant immortality, the artist was a kind of holy being. For the poor, with heaven's gate shut and without the money to commission a canvas simulacrum, there was no escape from oblivion.

The artist's principle role would be as explainer of bourgeois power, magically dispelling objections to the insanity, inequality, and hypocrisy of the new system. Before the Renaissance, the painter, musician, or sculptor was a craftsman; afterward, as an "artist," he was a seer and priest, anointed by his bourgeois patron. His work would elucidate his master's logic to the exploited masses. The artist was essentially a shock trooper for the capitalist's ideological indoctrinations.

The art-maker was therefore different from other

workers, both far above and far below them. This resulted in a deep state of alienation from society—its mores, ethics, clothes, and sleep schedule. In return for championing the master's god status on Earth, the artist could be interred as a legend after death. This status was always at the whim of the artist's employer, though; just as the bourgeoisie had created him, so could they dispose of him.

The artist as holy man was just one of many inventions commissioned by the capitalist, of course. The capitalist's greatest victory was his commission of the atom or "A-bomb"; that's when he really arrived. The single most compelling argument for the elite as living deities, after all, would be if they could appropriate God's best threat: Armageddon.

Beyond the Michelin restaurants, the private jets, and the high-priced brothels, the believable threat of Armageddon is what makes the capitalist a true potentate. Therefore, the threat of apocalypse must not only be a constant, but must also transform constantly, lest the public become inured to a familiar menace.

Acid rain, mutually assured destruction, killer bees, Ebola virus, Y2K, reactor meltdowns, global warming—capitalism demands not only constructed enemies and constructed desires, but also real impending crisis which threatens the human race itself with extinction. Terrorist threats and the threat of hurricanes, storms, tsunamis, and earthquakes are now conflated, so that weather itself is a terrorist.

The narcissistic idea of apocalypse and Armageddon

based on "fear of missing out" is something as old as mankind; it's difficult for each successive generation to imagine a world without them as its center. But only under capitalism are the cycles of seasons, generations, and the future itself absolutely unimaginable.

IV. THE ARTIST AS VAMPIRE

The artist is often identified as a kind of "vampire": carnal, callous, shape-shifting, nocturnal, undercover, possessing a strange, malevolent charisma, but ultimately parasitic.

The vampire myth started in the eighteenth century in Eastern Europe, an area which has had a third world relationship to the West ever since the Crusades. The Crusades weren't only an invasion of the Holy Land but also included colonization of the Baltic states and the sack of Constantinople, the grand seat of Eastern Christianity. Seen as a whole, the Crusades were principally an attempt by the Roman Church to colonize the East.

The countries of the East, having never experienced their own bourgeois revolutions, were—and still are—used by the West as resources and markets to be colonized. As a result, the people there immediately fostered suspicion of the artists who were heralds of a new invading class of exploiter.

The vampire legend, popular throughout Eastern Europe, was a manifestation of the fear of the new artist class and of the artist's portraits. The portrait painters were creating an immortal image, immortalizing their subjects, and becoming immortal themselves with their signatures, which—since the Renaissance—had become a feature of their work.

In the East, there had been a great fear of people immortalizing themselves, outside of the domain of God. God was, after all, the only one who could grant immortality. The portrait painters were committing blasphemy in that they were helping someone live forever outside of the aegis of God. Therefore, the portrait painter was, to Christians, apostate. There is a cliché of certain aboriginal peoples believing that the camera will steal one's soul. The portrait painter of yore likewise was seen as a soul-stealer or vampire.

The East had historically been suspicious of portraiture and the immortalization of a person. The famous "iconoclast" struggles of the Middle Ages—which centered around destruction of graven images—had torn apart the Orthodox Church in the ninth century, leading to a disruption which allowed the Vatican to break free of Byzantine authority, and which led to the East-West schism, a defining feature of modern times.

The struggle between Western-Catholic and Eastern-Orthodox is the backdrop to imperial conflicts such as the NATO bombing and dismemberment of Yugoslavia, World War II, and the US-designed conflict in Ukraine. In these struggles, capitalist powers like NATO and the Nazis typically fight on the side of the Catholics while the Communists, Serbs, or pro-Russian separatists are usually Orthodox-affiliated. Dracula was a story appropriated by author Bram Stoker from the myths and folk traditions of Slavic countries. Stoker set his story in Romania, but it could have taken place anywhere in the East.

Vampirism is a poignant condition not just because it is sexy and scary, but because the vampire is a victim too. The "Nosferatu" is a bloodthirsty creature who looks for prey, but he too was a victim once, a hapless dupe seduced by a thirsty immortal undead. This poignantly illustrates the conundrum faced by the artist under capitalism.

V. THE ARTIST AS GHOST

Art is often seen as a conjuring up, or as a message from the creator itself.

The musician or painter often complains of their fingers or pen (or whatever) being manipulated as if by ghosts, who lead them to the discovery or exhumation of what becomes their greatest hit. Keith Richards's riff for "(I Can't Get No) Satisfaction" is just one example.

An artist's stature often increases exponentially after they die, which isn't so strange when one considers that perhaps, once the artist has shaken off their mortal coil, all their energy can be focused on their career. Their artwork, whether it's a record, book, or painting, is thenceforth their only material manifestation, and thus, as opposed to the typical haunting of an old house, diving board, or stairway, the artist's ghost settles into their work.

Records and art are used as mediums with which to communicate to the "other side." Old records are, in a sense, our communion with the dead. Records blurt out trapped moments of rapture, fear, love, anguish, despair, excitement, and insanity. When an album plays, it is a ghost wailing, imprisoned in the moment, rattling its chains. Groups' graven images and output are likewise ghostlike, attempting to wreak their vision on the world from the afterlife, but without a physical body, they must rely on real-world minions, not unlike Stoker's Dracula, whose insane slave "R.M. Renfield" caught flies in the asylum while worshipping his beloved count. Every fan is ultimately a little Renfield, who alternately raves and obscures their fave group or record—that which they see as the light and hope for the Earth but also their precious, personal, esoteric discovery.

When a rock group begins, it mimics the rattle from some tragic old ghost of renown, and attempts to recreate its heroics; reenacting some momentary tantrum which was trapped forever on a vinyl disc. The artist's painting is rectangular and self-contained, but a record is round and—forever revolving—seems to move quickly, but actually goes nowhere. The record being sheathed in a square-shaped cover or jacket is a craven attempt to mimic fine art's rectangularity, and therefore ingratiate itself to the linear, orderly world of bourgeois respectability. Ovals and curves are, after all, linked to tribalism, pantheism, magic, and preindustrial mandalas. The record jacket gives the disc an outward appearance of being complete, systematic, anchored, and logical, so as to disguise the dark drama of the captured soul which rotates eternally in a gyre.

The song, as a bizarre circular repetition, is another flirtation with death and its bedfellow, insanity. The recorded group might live a long life, but once it has been recorded, it's a walking undead, tethered to a material manifestation of a particular moment in time that it must repeat again and again. Some groups go unnoticed and fail; ultimately, they are the ones who are free. Successful groups are like legendary ghosts who have to perform some stunted emotional moment for their entire lives and then on into death.

Record collectors' houses often feel a bit haunted. The collector is someone who consorts with ghosts and the supernatural quite regularly. The compulsion to find the value of an out-of-print record is an unconscious attempt to please the ghost trapped in the groove. They are often insecure about the worth of their contributions, and want terrestrial confirmation.

The recording process is a conjuring of magic, therefore, and as such is regarded suspiciously by some who are less rooted in capitalism's gizmo-conjuring production paradigm.

VI. THE ARTIST AS NUCLEAR RADIATION

Sometimes groups refuse to write songs or record, such as Pussy Riot from Russia, whose inspiration came from performance artists, the CIA, and the fanzines of the nineties US feminist punk-revival underground—as opposed to its music.

Those fanzines were, in part, inspired by the group Nation of Ulysses, which had a fanzine/newsletter proclaiming itself a political-terrorist party. Pussy Riot, the

Russian protest performance group, took this concept—the group as terrorist political theater—and their name from this riot grrrl faction of the nineties US punk revival. Their guerrilla theater—and the outsized reaction to it—was highly effective in turning world opinion against the Russian state.

The vampirism practiced by the US state in co-opting the "group as terrorist-political organization" via its sponsorship of front group Pussy Riot is a predictable version of its usual bloodsucking appropriation. Yet, since they don't make records, Pussy Riot are not yet dead and therefore have real potential to wreak the nuclear apocalypse long promised by the rock bands who, wailing from another dimension, have thus far been delinquent and ineffectual in their delivery.

It's no coincidence that Pussy Riot, who are hero/celebrities in the West and party with camp Catholic Madonna, began their struggle with the desecration of an Orthodox church in Moscow. Pussy Riot are the central pieces in the current push to suppress and recolonize the East, stars of the West's propaganda campaign against Russian president Vladimir Putin. They are the exemplary rationalization to liberals for the possibly armed confrontation with the Russian state, which the West elite despises for its gas wealth, otherness, and relative autonomy, as opposed to EU governments who are supplicant bootlicks to US-led neoliberal hegemony.

Pussy Riot, more than anyone ever, are the embodiment of the pure rock 'n' roll promise: they produce nothing, they do nothing, and are—to their audience—incomprehensible; yet they may have engendered a world war through a gesture of nihilistic defiance. In explaining and creating a framework for liberals to applaud US intervention against Russia, an isolated, resentful, and possibly desperate nuclear power, these artists have attained the apocalyptic god status typically reserved for the most elite bourgeoisie. In this manner, they might be the most powerful artists ever.

Pussy Riot are a singular group and cannot be enlisted to play a festival or join a package tour, as they have no real songs, records, or show. Per the rock 'n' roll archetype of absolute individualism, they are alone; isolated from other bands, from their nation, from everyone except the neoliberal celebrities who see them as the path to an easy activism with no negative social or commercial consequences; the best way to self-righteously shake one's fist since "Free Tibet" was the toast of the town.

10

HEATHERS REVISITED

THE NERD'S FIGHT FOR NICENESS

MASS SHOOTINGS HAVE PLAGUED the US in the years following the 1989 launch of the film *Heathers,* starring Winona Ryder and Christian Slater, which instructed the population that murdering popular people was a sexy, funny, and totally "gonzo" thing to do.

In the film, Winona Ryder's character Veronica Sawyer collaborates in killing her Westerburg High School tormentors—three girls all named Heather—with dark-horse new kid in town J.D. Dean, played by Christian Slater. The Heathers are slaughtered along with their football-star boyfriends. The murders are treated as just comeuppance, hilarious desserts served hot to Hollywood's typical WASP antagonists by dark-haired anti-heroes. This trope is repeated ad nauseam in American cinema (e.g., *The Graduate, Revenge of the Nerds, Addams*

Family, etc.). Besides Nazis, WASPs are Hollywood's reliable punching bag; the two are typically—for obvious reasons—conflated.

Heathers, a hit when it came out, was recently relaunched as a major Broadway production. Like *Hairspray, Grease,* and *The Lion King, Heathers* has become a beloved American fable.

In fact, the film was perhaps as influential to Americans as the Manson murders in promulgating domestic assassination of apolitical, everyday people as a revolutionary act. Just as Manson's "family" butchered high-powered hairdressers and starlets in a misguided attempt to spur apocalypse, the *Heathers* protagonists are geek-guardian guerrillas toppling the ruling class. In the film, after Winona's first assassination, she explains her intent: "I just want my high school to be a nice place." As political ideology and class consciousness are verboten in the United States, Americans now see execution of "mean" people as politically heroic. Army operatives in foreign countries explain their violence as "getting the bad guys." Before a hit on a foreign leader, the media regales us with stories of their personal cruelty. It's an activist model which has resulted in myriad casualties. What does this "niceness" constitute? In *Heathers* it seems to constitute a male-dominated social order and a latent Christianity.

That some young people, raised with the *Heathers* lesson, may have acted upon it so literally is, of course, horrifying. The assassins at Columbine, Virginia Tech, Aurora, etc., all apparently imagined they were striking out against a society which had hurt their feelings; they were therefore justified, like Winona's character Veronica Sawyer, in committing mass carnage. Whether they saw the film or not, its message has permeated the culture. What the killers didn't understand was that the film wasn't instructing its audience to wreak homicidal vengeance for some imagined slight. It is an allegory about the ascendancy of Christian patriarchal power. *Heathers* is an instruction manual, but the lesson is teaching Christians how to throw off the feminine yoke, not for nerds on how to go about mass murder.

The film begins with the three Heathers, deities who rule over a Gaia Earth-mother goddess realm. They are determining the course of human destiny in a magical game of croquet. This game is not only an elaborate ceremony prescribing mankind's fate but also a ritual to explicate power dynamics within the divine Heathers clique. There are three Heathers (Heather Chandler, Heather McNamara, and Heather Duke) just as there were three female "Norns" in Germanic-Norse mythology, three "Moirai" in Greek religion, three "Sudice" of Slavic legend, and three witches in *Macbeth.* The motif of a trio of female characters ("Fates") who callously determine humanity's fate (often through weaving) is pan-religious, shared by most Indo-European pagan cults.

These characters typically precede the establishment gods and goddesses; the Norns, for example, may have predated the Norse pantheon of Thor and Odin, et al, though they were integrated into the Valhalla myths as an arcane, all-powerful coterie. Even Odin, king of the gods, had to submit to the fate-spinning of the Norns. Belief in the Norns also survived in Scandinavia long after Christianity took over. Since the Heathers are these kinds of creatures, "Que Sera, Sera"—a song about accepting one's destiny—is used as the film's theme music.

The Heathers are rarely interacted with by the Westerburg High School student body, though they are feared, admired, and loathed. All powerful, they are bitchy, vindictive, and committed to their primitive religion of beauty, cruelty, and haughtiness. Winona/Veronica is their envoy and plays tricks on the nerds of the student body to appease them. But like a proto–Kurt Cobain, Veronica—despite being the high priestess of the Heathers—is ambivalent about the religion she represents and its rigid power structure.

When J.D. Dean, the son of a construction mogul, arrives at school, he and Veronica start dating. They perform a sex-magick ritual on the sacred croquet field so as to undo the fema-talitarian state which the Heathers have constructed. The couple's murder spree begins soon thereafter with the chief Heather (Heather Chandler) as their first victim. She is poisoned after a night of drinking and sodomizing at a college party. Veronica and Heather had fallen out over the former rejecting the sexual advances of a college man.

After poisoning the chief goddess, J.D. and Veronica kill the high school's football stars Ram and Kurt, oafish male guardians of the Heathers order. They are murdered for spreading saucy rumors involving themselves and Veronica in an "oral ménage." Their sacrifice is performed at night in a circle of magick, while they are naked and defenseless. In death, the footballers are smeared as closeted homosexuals. Just as Heather Chandler's sluttiness made her killing acceptable, Ram and Kurt's horny libel and polymorphous perversity makes them ritual-sacrifice fodder. J.D. and Veronica are indicting the Heatherian world as decadent, unnatural, and sin-ridden, similar to the Christian characterization of Roman pagans as sodomite perverts.

At this point in the story, J.D.'s father, Big Bud Dean, is introduced. He walks in on Veronica and J.D. as they ridicule Heather's funeral on TV. J.D. represents Christ in the film, and his father God. They communicate to one another in reverse, the father as the son and the son as the father; a displacement designed to show they are the same. The God/father is a real estate developer/construction mogul. As such, he is a destroyer of the old order. In erecting the new, he is confronted with historic preservationists—all female—who he describes as "withered old bitches," and who comprise pagan-sounding organizations such as the Save the Memorial Oak Tree Society. His success against them is ineluctable.

The father's description of his demolition of a historic hotel is a premonition of a 9/11 conspiracy: "I put a Norwegian in the boiler room. Masterful. And then when that blew, it set off a pack of thermals I stuck upstairs." It turns out a similar "controlled demolition" had already eradicated J.D.'s mother. This God is the Old Testament God, a famously vindictive, malevolent, and sadistic character.

In the wake of the student bloodbath, feminine forces make a last stand back at the school to try to rally the esprit de corps of the Heathers dominion. A hippie she-teacher at Westerburg sponsors a schoolwide hug-in to the soundtrack of fictional band Big Fun's megahit "Teenage Suicide (Don't Do It)." This is the desperate death rattle of the femme-talitarian ideology. The lowliest Heather, Heather Duke, is obsessed with premonitions of the inevitable ascension of male supremacists. She is always reading Melville's *Moby Dick* about the fearsome phallic leviathan. By the end, she has converted to J.D.'s side.

As the murders create mayhem at the school, Veronica complains about the chaos. But J.D. explains: "Chaos is great! Chaos is what killed the dinosaurs, darling! Face it, our way is the way!" For the Christian, chaos preceded "the way" (*The Way* is the name of a famous Opus Dei manual and a euphemism for Christianity). The God/father emerges from this chaos, and the Christ/son is "the way," the path out of disorder. The mother/sister/female gods of paganism are disposed of in monotheism, therefore requiring the famous "virgin birth," which ensures a nondivine status for Mary.

Christian Slater's performance in this film was dismissed by critics as channeling Jack Nicholson too blatantly. These hacks didn't understand that he was actually *playing* Jack Nicholson, who had been cast as the devil in

Witches of Eastwick two years before (1987). In this explanation of Christianity, rebel Lucifer and Son of God are blurred as one; they represent the new forces of maleness and Christianity. Veronica, as the reluctant priestess of the goddess religion, speaks to her father in a mantra refuting paternal authority. "You're an idiot," she incessantly reminds him. This abuse is meted out because he is a neutered man of the woman-ruled pagan world. Her superiority complex melts away in the face of J.D.'s new macho paradigm.

As funerals are held for Veronica's victims, each Heather or Heather cohort who is murdered haunts her. She resents their postmortem characterizations as "nice." They were not "nice"! As a born-again Christian, Veronica needs to ensure that the old ways aren't just discontinued but eradicated from the collective memory, as were the druids, witches, and medicine men of pagan Europe and America. "Heather Chandler is more popular than ever now," J.D. laments after her murder. Memory is a threat to the institutionalization of the new religion. With J.D.'s spectacular crucifixion/martyrdom at the movie's climax, patriarchal monotheism is firmly installed at Westerburg High.

The high school is named for Paul Westerberg of rock band the Replacements, since the story is about one power "replacing" another. "There's a new sheriff in town," Veronica declares at the end of the film. *Heathers* is a simple story about the victory of patriarchal monotheism/ Christianity over feminine paganism in antiquity, and an

TASS PHOTO VIA UPI

(*Top*) Georgi Beregovoy in an October 29 telecast from Soyuz 3. (*Bottom*) The widow, left, of first spaceman Yuri Gagarin, killed in a March 27 plane crash,, is solaced by former cosmonaut Valentina Nikolayeva-Tereshkova.

exhortation for Christians to overthrow castrating feminine power. The unremarkable Slater was obviously cast as J.D. for his name—"Christian"—while "Heather" is a plant, used as a sacrament by pagans who supposed it to possess magical properties. "Ryder" means a knight, who fights for their liege lord. Meanwhile, a "sawyer" is a cutter of wood, and "slater" means "roofer." Fitting, as these two are in the process of building a new church for a new world.

Unfortunately, *Heathers* isn't understood for what it is. It has been misinterpreted as a pro–mass murder film; a *Catcher in the Rye* for the nerd-berserk, an inspirational guide for the grumpy and the maladjusted. And in an alienated individualist country like the USA, that includes everyone. The USA is a nation of 300 million–plus potential lone-nut gunmen.

Or perhaps not. Mass killings in the States are overwhelmingly—though not exclusively—performed by white men, possibly harboring some grievance that their superiority or sexiness hasn't been recognized. *Heathers* is the story of the violent destruction of feminine power, of those bitches who thought they were so hot. The sexual component of gun violence correcting impotence is obvious, as is the patriarchal desire for name immortality (if not through progeny, then via infamy). This is the subtext to much of the post-*Heathers* violence epidemic.

In 1969, the Manson murders transfixed and horrified a public inured to violence by TV's nightly Vietnam War body counts because the Family seemed so "mean."

They were girls who were dirty, scuzzy, scrawled bloody graffiti on walls, and murdered a well-liked film actress. Carving swastikas into their foreheads, they took on the role of supervillains. Their acts resonated not just because of a latent fear of the hippie menace or fascination with lurid gore, but because people could relate to the Family's simplistic idea of political struggle—a Wild West kind of vigilante justice—just not their chosen targets or precise methods. That seemed incontrovertibly "mean." Conversely, twenty years later, the celluloid *Heathers* protagonists were applauded because their spree was fomenting the ideology of "niceness."

Technically, *Heathers* features a pair of serial killers as opposed to mass murderers, or perhaps a pair of serial-spree killers (mass murder being a single incident, spree killing being a few immediately related incidents, and serial killing being several murders committed over time, according to the FBI, which has committed lots of each), whereas the headline-grabbing killers of today are typically mass murderers. *Heathers'* influence still reverberates; it is a film on par with *Birth of a Nation, Gone with the Wind, Star Wars,* and *Titanic* in capturing and shaping the attitudes of its age.

Each one of America's mass killers is a psychotic malcontent who, in a different age, might possibly have put their rage to some constructive use. Their crimes are misguided acts of political nihilism. This is the fallout of the ideology of the pop-psych pharma-state. With everything reduced to predestination/DNA by the drug-industry propaganda machine, a pill is the answer to one's problems, not transformation of one's goals or circumstances. With the entrenched belief that political radicalism or analysis will remove one from the dating pool, few in the USA dare examine the root of their despair. If the pills don't work, the only answer is to go out in a blaze of glory.

As with the Manson killers, the modern lone-nut imagines his deeds are akin to Che Guevara battling in the Sierra Maestra. But, since the social law of the country circumscribes political thought, instead of an articulated ideology (i.e., in the case of Che, ending Cuba's status as a US corporate-owned, racially segregated plantation state) or a plan (wealth redistribution, for example), the only intent is for revenge against the "mean" people who did them "wrong." Fighting for the cause of "niceness."

In the early seventies, when copycat crime sprees broke out following the release of Kubrick's adaptation of *A Clockwork Orange,* author Anthony Burgess responsibly helped to ban his own creation in England so as to halt such antisocial behavior. He recognized the power of art—particularly the moving image—to shape our world and our minds. Though Winona Ryder and Christian Slater could use their power as supercelebrities to caution people against a violent endorsement of their film, no one involved with *Heathers* has ever stepped forward to make such a statement.

PART III

TRUTH IS NOT INVITED TO THE ORGY

SUPPRESSION AS EXPRESSION

[The actual writings comprising Part III were all lost and the ideas forgotten. The only trace of their having existed were a few marker scrawlings on a crumpled napkin. An attempt was made to recreate the ideas based on this evidence, and the punctuation and paragraphing have been preserved as best as possible. —The Author]

11

THE SERVICE INDUSTRY

WHEN ONE TRAVELS, one can see the origins of modern tipping. A tipped service in a foreign land is one typically performed by someone who is not an employee of an establishment but works either as an adjunct or as a free agent (e.g., a shoeshine boy). In a "third world" city, a self-styled tour guide might be tipped in return for leading a group of sightseers. Or in Italy, a Neapolitan street urchin might offer to protect one's parked car in return for a gratuity.

In both cases, the inference is clear: if you don't employ me (albeit momentarily), I will hurt you, since you are vulnerable due to your property and concern for decorum. This thinly veiled extortion is the subtext to much tipping: if the propertied individual doesn't comply with the demands of the semiemployed, something terrible might happen to them or their things. So tipping began essentially as a way to stave off violence by the indigent; a social contract adhered to by the privileged class who fear and disdain the less fortunate and are aware of their own class' failure to create equity.

But tipping or "gratuity" in the USA is something more nuanced. The people who are tipped in North America comprise an ever-expanding number of employed professions. Employers recognize the tipped individual as a great boon to the business—someone who needn't be given benefits, a wage, or employment security. They are essentially a guest at the business who must comport themselves appropriately for monetary reward courtesy of the customer. And this reward can be large. The tip, though it is a ghost fee, is actually a fairly strict number (15–20 percent of a tab, one dollar per drink, etc.), and is essentially mandatory; a failure to pay will result in public shaming or even fisticuffs. The tipping scale varies wildly and is determined by race and class factors. Cute, young white people are often given the desirable, highly visible jobs at restaurants and bars which tip well, while Central American immigrants work for trickle-down tips in the back.

In the USA, one is required to tip one's waiter, bartender, taxi driver, bellhop, coffee barista, sandwich artist, valet parker, coat check, hairdresser, barber, driver, masseuse, pedicurist, striptease artist, dog walker, hotel maid, concierge, delivery person, etc. A tipped job is typically one that is tied to a very quantifiable service done for a particular person or group. It is often linked to the idea of a "luxury" service as well (i.e., an espresso could be made at home so you must tip if you are buying it while out). In this sense it is maintained by the consumer as a self-punishing guilt fee.

Meanwhile, a bus driver on a daily route will not be tipped though he or she is working hard, serving the public. Policemen are not tipped except in the form of "donations" by fascist ass-kissers to a "fraternal order" in exchange for a bumper sticker, which apparently obtains preferential treatment for the driver in re: interactions with police. But in fact, besides this, public servants are not tipped. The tipped individual is providing a personal, *private* service.

Personal service is therefore the crux. Tipping is the onus of the purchaser who pays the wage of the worker on top of the cost of whatever service is provided, which goes to the business itself.

If one ever tries to discuss tipping in the USA one is immediately met with a dismissive and lofty: "Well, I tip really well because I was/am part of the service industry." Like veterans of the armed forces, the "service people" are bound together in a cult which has experienced the true nature of work servitude and the demeaning, harrowing experience it represents. The fellow warrior conspicuously tips very well in a great display of homage and respect. Service implies a subservience but also a noble sacrifice. The service industry prepares our sandwiches nobly, submitting to our personalized mayonnaise request. Almost all Americans have worked in the service industry at some point and many will only ever work there.

Tipping, for these service-industry comrades, is outside of money. It is an alm or genuflection; a gesture of humility to the tipee designed to recognize and rehabilitate the degrading nature of their work, and also to connect with them spiritually. The camaraderie and smile dispensed by the waitstaff on receiving a generous tip—after a suspenseful meal service—brings the light of spiritual nourishment to the tipper. He or she can rest well that night. The Napoli street urchin's implied violence still hovers over the interaction, but now the justice and retribution feel more karmic.

Just as oblations to the poor will puff up one's sense of self, "tipping well"—20 percent or more—is a measure of one's personal decency. People often boast of their tipping. The least attractive thing one could do in the USA is tip stingily. This is for old religious people or clueless foreigners. Conversely, if one leaves a tip at a coffee bar in parts of Europe, the barista looks insulted and confused, as if you were treating him or her as a beggar; "Are you some kind of playboy show-off who throws your money around?" Obviously these people never saw the Scorsese film *Goodfellas,* which portrays mafiosas in the sixties tipping wildly in a display of rampant virility.

People stumble over themselves to brag of their tipping prowess, and despite the inherent and obvious injustice of a massive, scarcely paid workforce scraping and begging for a wage, there has yet to be a true revolt of tipped employees. In a lottery-minded *American Idol* culture, workers are loathe to give up the chance for a Saudi sheikh to tip them a million dollars as a reward for preparing a great smoothie. And there are palpable dividends: tattooed bartenders are bad-boy sex symbols who determine who gets served and when. Their management gives them an allotment of courtesy drinks which they can hand out to high-tipping customers or prospective lovemaking partners. Their favor is therefore highly sought by bar-goers due to their high-handed, undemocratic authority.

Tipping therefore has many purposes besides being an exploitive business model. It either shows one's affinity for one's comrades in the service industry, or is a duty done reluctantly by the bourgeoisie to stave off insurrection. It absolves one of sins and wrongdoing, so it's religious. It is a guilt fee paid by the ill-conscienced for the immoral act of indulging in luxury. It is an act of dominance as it displays power via capital, and also an act of submission: a paid tribute offered to the serviceperson. All of this is erotic and exciting, which accounts for the huge popularity of tipping.

Tipping makes us into slaves and masters simultaneously in a confused, kinetic, and highly kinky social model. The service-industry model carries over into the bedroom with the modern emphasis on oral sex and "servicing" one's partner. And it is cross-cultural; the service industry in the postindustrial "West" accounts for most jobs: up to 80 percent in the USA (according to the World Bank), which has exported most of its industry to cheaper countries and mechanized its farms. In fact the USA, more than most nations, is almost entirely dualistic;

on one hand there is the bourgeoisie or "middle class," and on the other, the service industry.

But this binary is blurry. "Middle class" is a designation worn by all Americans except possibly some rappers who claim to be rich. Warren Buffett, for example, likely calls himself "middle class." Most in the service industry would likewise do so. Politicians pander to a mythic middle class in their stump speeches. Middle class, in the USA, has been stripped of its old meaning—owners of capital or wealthy, propertied nonaristocrats—and come to mean someone who is positioned in the middle, between the very richest person and the very poorest person. All but two people in the USA are middle class. (An interesting note: neither of these people are a junkie dying in a hospice or a tramp on the street; while the richest man is a faceless billionaire compiling hedge fund data, the poorest is a faceless ex-billionaire hedge funder down the street from him who, through a misplaced keystroke, is now steeped in incomprehensible debt.)

Of course, the idea of a middle class is not really one's bank balance but instead a set of values. It is a social group with concern for the results of their actions. "Middle Class" was an insult during a more class-conscious era, grumbled in France with proletarian disdain at those who bartered the present for an imagined future. Middle-class behavior included: investing in stocks, buying insurance, owning real estate, worshipping "work," loving science, and practicing austerity despite having wealth. Irreligious Protestantism, in short. Healthy eating, temperance, decorum, and sensible behavior are all "bourgeois" to a proletariat who revel in the moment, unfettered by concerns about interest rates and the "slow dime."

To the middle class, both the lower and upper class (titled aristocrats who have inherited their wealth) are despicable due to their disdain for work and the Protestant ethic, and for the guiltless joy they derive in sensual pleasure, such as drunkenness and fornication. Nations or communities which are poor or never had a bourgeois revolution are marked by orgies of revelry quite unknown in more economically prosperous places. These places are incomprehensible to the American sensibility which views them as savage, brutal, and insane (i.e., Russia, Africa, much of South America and Asia). The USA's foreign policy is essentially to make people American (via capitalism) or kill them. They are better off dead than living any other way.

The American Revolution was, of course, along with the French Revolution and the English civil wars, a Protestant/Masonic/capitalist revolution. It was, as much as the American/Israeli-propagated Middle East violence, a clash of socioreligious sensibilities. On one hand the Calvinist capitalists who worshipped industry, and on the other the clergy-allied landed gentry who saw work as man's curse. When the Masonic forces prevailed, it also ensured that a growth-oriented work ideology would prevail.

Though the capitalists in the USA were slave owners, who derived much of their wealth from forced, unpaid labor, they revered the concept of "work." They presented themselves as personally industrious, and from Jefferson's and Washington's achievements we can see that some of them were. Their revolution laid the groundwork for a nation which, in many respects, is still a work camp.

Called the "land of opportunity," the USA typically lures immigrants with the promise of making money, and not with the "enlightened" social values or the quality of life. When one goes to Brooklyn, the housing blocks and the trains remind one that New York City in the industrial era was essentially a concentration camp of foreign textile workers who, like many of the less visible employees in the service industry, were barely paid.

They too were placated by the idea of chance. The chance wages of the tip jar are mystical, undefined, practically psychedelic; therefore, they are more attractive than the cold, hard reality of the paycheck. The tip jar is thus a symbol of worker passivity. This modern condition of a giant impoverished "middle class" of service-industry workers conspicuously trading generous tips with one another in a prolonged orgy of self-congratulation and simulated affluence must end. As long as the dream world of nebulous "karma jar" income pollutes the atmosphere, no one can reconcile the insane injustice of an uncompensated labor force being paid through the guilty feelings of their coworkers.

Can you imagine 1920s steelworkers in Pittsburgh, their faces stained with soot and grime, paying each other's wages while their mill bosses pleaded poverty? That's essentially what's happening now in a merry-go-round circle jerk of dream economics. When the first barista refuses the enforced gesture of happy-go-lucky largesse by their off-of-work coworker, then the whole stinking system will collapse in a mound of idiocy and be revealed for the soft-core indentured servitude that it is.

12

MUSIC AND THE STRUGGLE AGAINST SANITY

THERE IS A SECRET LANGUAGE of dreams . . . you hear people speaking it in the dead of night when nestled under their covers. It uses just one letter—Z—and sounds something like "*Zzzzz.*"

Z is the end of the alphabet. Not only at the edge of sounds, but also of reason and meaning. It rubs provocatively against the unknown and attempts to barge into the next dimension. "Zzzzz" is the sound of the letter Z grinding stubbornly against the border of the alphabet in a bid to escape into pure, primordial, meaningless madness.

With all this snoring, the sleeping person fancies him or herself a surrealist crusader. But there is a valve each sleeper is built with which leashes them to "reality," resisting their desire to escape into the unknown. Otherwise they would drift away forever, and if awoken, they'd bring their dream logic into waking life. This could have unpredictable and perhaps dangerous results.

The sleeper is a strange breed of person, characterized by stubbornness, immobility, and a kind of idiocy. These people want to be "free," not only from the rules governing society but also the natural laws of gravity, time, space, et cetera. They want to be "insane." Their attempts at achieving this state always stall, however. Einstein supposedly said, "Doing the same action again and again and expecting different results is insane." Yet, while the sleeper goes to bed every night expecting different dreams and visions, he or she never really achieves true insanity. They just flirt with it until they are awoken, and bewilderingly recount a few half-remembered dream fragments. After this, they immediately forget everything, have a coffee, and enter the humdrum world of the waking. They are sellouts; assimilationists. These serial sleepers are a growing majority, though, as sleep medicines are more heavily prescribed and late-night television becomes less compelling.

The sleeper's poseur pretensions and lack of commitment to the crazy world they brush up against give them little credibility. They are like a yuppie "slumming," a marine at a punk show, or a tourist in an exotic land. Their brand of crazy is generally considered tedious, so much so that when something is banal or boring, people often mimic the sleeper's *"Zzzzz"* language as a repudiation.

There are other languages which more effectively approach madness. There is the language of love and pleasure, for example, spoken entirely in vowels—*"Aaa," "Uuu,"* and *"Ooo"*—which is closely related to the language of fear and horror—*"EEeeeE!!!"*—and also to the language of harmonic music.

Music is in the same language group as dreams, pleasure, love, and fear, and is characterized by the letters E, A, D, G, B, F, C, B#, and so on; letters which denote chords and notes.

Like the language of sleep and dreams, music is another attempt to transport the listener to a place where normal logic doesn't apply. Voltaire's "Anything too stupid to be said is sung" could also be, "If it doesn't make sense, it can be a song." Songs defy logic, sense, proper storytelling, and the modern rock 'n' roll group is typically a bundle of inanity when performing onstage. They rarely induce dancing and are often loathe to "perform" in any way that would traditionally be thought of as entertaining. Country music, a format which usually insists on a narrative arc for its song-stories, is therefore considered corny, kitsch, out-of-date, and ridiculous. Groups with a coherent "show," who attempt to communicate with an audience, are similarly dismissed as old fashioned. Audiences now want the surreal, the scary, the "insane." They want to enter into a dream world where groups either stomp about under strange light displays wearing outlandish costumes or affect ridiculous nonchalant understatement whilst muttering non sequitur absurdities, as with "indie" music.

Songs are used in shopping malls, on the campaign trail during political elections, on the battlefield during war, and for mind-control purposes when "courting" would-be paramours. All these are situations in which good sense, sobriety, and logic are the sworn enemies of the one utilizing the tunes. Music "tames the wild breast," but is this through calm and reason? No, this is because "wild" is a relative term and music is simply more deranged, nonsensical, and "wild" than whatever it's being compared to.

Indeed, music is often explicitly insane. The shouts and screams of rock 'n' roll music, the strange repetition of lyrics, the ridiculous, overwrought gymnastics of vocal chords, the outsize emotions, and the surrealism of psychedelia are only appropriate for the stage. If someone were to be seen behaving like a musician outside of the specifically designated stage zone, that person would be committed or drugged into oblivion by concerned doctors.

Therefore, the music performer's stage is a mini–insane asylum. The performers on it are encouraged—nay required—to make calamitously loud music, to scream, shout, and flail in a bizarre display, all the while moaning about love, unhappiness, or something mumbled and therefore incomprehensible. Though rock 'n' roll began as pure insanity, with nonsense words ("Wop bop a doo wop," "Be bop a lula," "Rama lama ding dong"), its modern model is even more crackers. Whatever melody or cogency that once was present in, for example, a Chuck Berry song, has been obliterated. It is thought to be too typical, too normal. Now, ever more psychotic effects (fuzz, reverb, delay, compression, samples) are commandeered to obfuscate and bury any discernible tune or theme.

Though music is more effective than sleep in approximating the freedom of madness, it is still extraordinarily limited in its war against sanity. The chords and notes that it has in its quiver are only a few, and it must make do with arranging them again and again into the same few formations to achieve what it must. Though music seems to be ubiquitous, and therefore victorious in its struggle for total chaos, it is actually locked in pitched combat with a vast array of forces who support chaos' ancient enemy—"control."

Music's enemies, the "control" group, include schools, parents, teachers, government, grammar, work, police, the armed forces, the DMV, regulatory commissions, grant writers, professional and amateur sports leagues, arts councils, architects, physicists, the space program, and almost everything and everybody else. Though many of these institutions seem even more insane than music, they all fight for a normative ideology. For example, the army wants to kill, maim, explode, and annihilate. It trains people to dress in green and hunt human beings. Its hierarchy, clothing styles, argot, and self-mythologizing are as strange and terrifying as anything one might witness in a lunatic asylum overcome by cannibalism. But according to the accepted societal framework, the army is a perfectly respectable bureaucracy; people wear *Army* sweatshirts and put *Army* stickers on their bumper. Its economic power and self-preservation instincts make it—despite much damning evidence—"classifiably sane."

As music fights against powerful institutions such as

the army and football, it must sometimes array itself on a field of combat. Not coincidentally, the tablature for chords as they appear on a guitar fret board resemble the strategic battle maps in army HQ or a ball coach's charts for running plays.

Sports games are often likened to mock combat; a gladiatorial stand-in for the fractious interstate disagreement of war. The rock 'n' roll group also attempts to simulate such struggles of blood and iron, with their "Battle of the Bands" contests and their hit-parade charts designating winners and losers. Apologists for music insist that it's a different thing altogether, that it's not a contest and that everything is absolutely subjective. But if one looks at the aforementioned fret board, the chords tell a different tale.

Seen in this manner, the A chord is quite intimidating. All three notes stand in a line guarding the fret board. It's a traditional phalanx, a defensive posture. Its affect is guarded; the sound invokes the nervous drinking of rationed whiskey, popping of amphetamines, and pensive waiting for the command to attack. "A" guards the "home base" of the headstock. This base is the place from whence all chord attacks originate, as they drive down the "field" of the fret board toward the "sound hole" or pickups, depending on whether the instrument is acoustic or electrified.

The E chord is the company or regiment on a bivouac. Its ringing, open strings convey a sense of breezy confidence. With E, the campaign seems to be going smoothly; either a "sitzkrieg" or a "cakewalk." With E, the intimation is that the squad has just spent time at the officer's drinking hole or has given out some chocolate bars to war orphans. They're feeling good about themselves. The E chord is the archetype rock 'n' roll and blues chord. It's the most common primordial rock 'n' roll chord and as such it represents a kind of "status quo." E minor is this chord but with just a skeleton crew manning the post.

The D chord, meanwhile, is a flanking movement, up toward some tender and juicy exposed flaw in the enemy's armor. It's a chord which evokes a victorious commando strike. A minor is a chord which is dark and wounded. The position on the fret board shows that there has been a setback from the A defensive position, either a retreat of the unit or lots of wounded or destroyed soldiery. A minor is prevalent in Gothic music.

And so on. Most rock 'n' roll songs comprise three chords and are arranged as a I-IV-V progression, meaning that the chords used have this 1-4-5 relationship relative to one another. The song "Louie, Louie," which caused great concern to the control group when it stormed the charts, is configured in this way, and could be played with the chords A, D, Em, D, and back to A, for example. This represents a military-style maneuver, starting with the aggressive but conservative A chord, with all the troops lined up, then going "over the top" with the heroic D, and ending back eventually at A.

The chords configured against the forces of order have been arranged over the years again and again, with usually predictable, ho-hum results. But occasionally a tiresomely familiar pattern, typically in this 1-4-5 arrangement, will catch the enemy off guard, and break open a hole in the bulwark constructed by the combined forces of boringness, decorum, idiocy, dullness, television, fear, bureaucracy, patriotism, et cetera. Once the defensive position is pierced, the chords and notes of disorder pour into the wound like an overeager swarm of bacteria on a fresh wound. And order is defeated . . . Or is it?

Thus far, not quite. Despite many victories of sound, countless hours of recorded music which confuses, bewilders, stuns, and stupefies, control holds the upper hand. It seems that once the victorious chord configuration shoves its way into fearsomely lame enemy territory, it finds itself ingratiated to its new surroundings. Instead of keeping up the fight, it quickly assimilates. Instead of terrorizing the squares, it is peacefully domesticated. "Louie, Louie," once considered the scourge of the Earth with its indecipherable lyrics, is now grazing peacefully at the baseball game. "Anarchy in the UK" is used to sell zit cream and automobile insurance.

In fact, it is in victory that music betrays its pledge to wreak insanity. When music is firmly ensconced in a basement or garage or seared onto a crusty cassette tape or musty 45, it retains its promise to be the bridge to another world. But in success it loses its ardor. As with the barbarian hordes who used to periodically conquer the Forbidden City, the urge is to lay down the banner and take up with the emperor. To exploit gain, after all, would hardly be insane. It would be the essence of good sense and predictability.

Of course, war is a two-way street. To characterize the conflict as a one-sided action, with music doing all the pummeling, is unfair. Especially to those musicians who have been brutalized by reason for so long. And it isn't only the practitioners who are the victims, but music itself. The forces of pragmatism have made many attempts to crush, corral, and utilize music for their own ends, in sometimes startling ways.

Indeed, the forces of reaction and control have set up their camp deep in music's territory through institutions such as ASCAP, BMI, Universal, BMG, WEA, *American Bandstand, Rolling Stone* magazine, iTunes, *Pitchfork,* and Clear Channel. But other challenges to music's pledged insanity are more insidious.

One example of the covert war between music and government would be the folk revival movement (1946–1964). This was thought up by the US government as a mission of cultural voyeurism and imperialistic co-opting. Bean-counting federal song collectors attempted to cull and classify every exotic backwoods jingle, copyright it, and give it a Latin name, like scientists on the HMS *Beagle.* They even lured real musicians—who came to be called folkies or "folkniks"—to participate, who were unaware of the orderly nature of the project.

Folkies mistakenly saw their work as activism (considered by society at the time to be "insane"), and many were intimately involved in organizations such as CND and SNCC, and went on "Freedom Rides" down south. Pete Seeger was sent to prison for Communist sympathies after resisting McCarthy's HUAC investigations, while Paul Robeson traveled on goodwill missions to the USSR where he was dosed with LSD by the CIA in an attempt to discredit him in front of his Russian comrades.

Folk music became an ideological battleground for the soul of the nation, between the competing forces of chaos and control. The folkniks might have had the best of intentions but what they really served to do was compile all manner of songs into music books to be reused, free of charge, by mostly English rock stars, to conquer the known music world. Listeners, unaware of the origins of the tunes, understandably assumed that these new troubadours, with long hair and velvet trousers, were lunatic savants, with limitless imagination, committed to combating sanity and boringness. Actually, they were pilfering a few centuries of working-class and slave traditions, neatly compiled by earnest song collectors like Harry Smith and the Almanac Singers.

Fads of the 1960s, like folk music, protests, Edwardian fashion, and hitchhiking, were in large part a retro-revival of Great Depression lifestyles; paradoxical, since the swinging sixties were the pinnacle of wealth and ease in America. Rock 'n' roll seemed to be the perfect delivery system to make the world go totally bonkers, with its dance "crazes" like the ostrich, bird, frug, shimmy, mashed potato, hully gully, etc. But by the end of the sixties, the forces of bourgeois practicality had reined in rock's real nature with the stadium trend. People were now sitting around, smoking dope, aping the most tedious members of straight society.

With rock 'n' roll beset by these ideologically impure agents of the sane world, it becomes less and less a dependable source of craziness. Much of its mania is now suspect and the average group must be looked upon as possible infiltrators, like a lone GI soldier encountered during the Battle of the Bulge. Indeed, the average group's rude gestures against the square world seem halfhearted at best, and at worst, infantile posturing by pro-sanity counterspies and turncoats. The promise of rock 'n' roll, which once seemed to be committed entirely to bringing an end to bourgeois tedium, now seems like a faint hope. Many of the faithful have already turned in their membership cards.

Of course, music mustn't be too harshly condemned for its history of failure. One consideration is the definition of sanity. Sanity, as we have discussed before, is an arbitrary set of standards regarding decorum and values which is foisted on us by the ruling clique. Meanwhile, though the absorption of music into the mainstream of society is depressing, we must trust that it still makes its mark. The squares who hum "Louie, Louie" while mowing the lawn don't realize that the song is working its spell on them. While it seems to have lost all its power, its values of imbalance and nonsense actually persist. Just as the barbarian invasions slowly changed the Roman Empire, music's repeated storming of the citadel of good sense has worn it down and transformed it indubitably. Heroic forays into its tender innards have infected control's body and mutated it. It is more susceptible than ever to attacks against its values of propriety and levelheadedness. Music, the weapon of imbalance and derangement, may yet triumph.

I AM SORRY, BUT YOU WILL NEVER SEE HIM AGAIN! BEFORE HE DIED... HE CONTACTED ME
ALTER

13

NOTES ON CAMP *PTS. II & III*

II. POP

IN THE SIXTIES, Andy Warhol declared war on the academy by promulgating "Pop Art"; the idea that comics, commercial labels, and industrial logos were art. This new "art movement" was applauded by a philistine population who had long felt insulted and browbeaten by cultural elites who summered in Paris embracing difficult European abstraction and the radical avant-garde. Pop began as painted logos but soon spread to include Warhol's mass media endeavors: film, prints, happenings, and sculpture.

Warhol's early films, seen as interminable, boring, and detached, were just simple, unadorned transmissions of a stoned experience; the psychedelic equivalent to entries in a ship's log or the dry observances of Che Guevara's diary. *Chelsea Girls* and *The Exploding Plastic Inevitable* were surrealist drug trips for the casual onlooker; attempting to explain the "high" consciousness to a straight participant. Pop Art is a sophomoric, stoned equivocation: mass produced objects as living beings . . . and vice versa.

More than Warhol's films, TV shows, magazine, and events, this latter proposal continues to resonate; indeed it seems more and more poignant. Pop—a.k.a. the assembly line—was, to the alienated postwar consumer, like a dazzling act of god. Or so it was designed to appear. Items from "The Factory," divorced as they were from the craftsman's hand, were imbued with something universal, timeless, perfect. Alienation of the workers from themselves, their labor, and the product of their labor, was, for the Pop-ist, a state of grace, not the tragedy that Marx had warned against.

Warhol's Pop was a declaration of love for these "goods," promulgating a new kind of romantic desire for a postwar generation whose ability to love other people was so stunted they had to enforce the dictum to "love" with signs, in songs, and on protest placards. They even declared a "Summer of Love" (May–August 1967), like a campaign to recycle or an end-of-season sale. Warhol's insistence on the personification of the commodity and the commodification of the person—as with his Marilyn portrait—neatly sums up the state of "l'amour" in the consumer capitalist society.

"Alienation of labor" was something that Marx had witnessed, with the pell-mell rise of capitalism and industrialization, in his own lifetime. It summed up the situation of the workers, who no longer had a direct relationship to the things that they made. But Marx lived in a time of revolutions and street actions; he saw the establishment of the Paris Commune as well as the revolutions of 1848 (the "Springtime of Peoples"), when people still felt they had agency to change their world. He couldn't have predicted the heights of alienation achieved by modern consumer culture.

This alienation has only been rehabilitated and made bearable by institutionalized drug use—legal and illegal—at every level of society. Though the drug culture purports to be a rebellion, it's actually state mandated and determined by the needs of imperial policy as well as by industry. The state's narcotic prohibition was just a clever move designed to make drug users feel empowered, special, and sexy—sort of like Facebook's early "college only" pretense.

The drug scene which shaped US culture in the sixties was a direct result of the compulsory addiction of conscripted soldiers in the army, enforced by the state. When the soldiers came home they wanted to keep feeling the "ups" and "downs" that had transformed their service into something more interesting.

Life in the army, after all, is incredibly boring, but it is also marked by a certain largesse: soldiers are encouraged to go whoring, engage in violence, and generally misbehave, so as to blow off steam accumulated while waiting for action that typically never comes. The soldier is an object with no value except for their ability to use money requisitioned for the military budget. They aren't required to do anything except consume (besides killing people during wartime, which is relatively unusual).

As drug culture in the USA had martial origins, it retained particular values when it was absorbed by the counterculture; it was colored by army life, army mentality, and army preoccupations. The California counterculture's main drug dealers, the Hells Angels, for example, had started life as bored itinerant ex–Air Force and, when discharged, had refused to give up the rapacious, "free" lifestyle they'd experienced bombing people overseas. The beatniks who were their customers also organized into militant "cell"-style cliques with vague insurrectionary ideologies.

Warhol's fabulous coterie were ex-debutantes and social strivers who provided a kind of USO to the drug-addled, deviant counterculture, serving up perverted in-jokes and Dada to a smashed, sophisticate audience.

"The Factory" was an ironic title in that drugs at the time were antiwork. Whether you dealt them or took them, they were an antidote to production. The true expression of a postindustrial consumer society.

It was a scene that got considerable publicity and became an inspiration to millions; the pill-popping hedonism of the "It Girl" and the other superstars in Andy's orbit.

III. CAMP

Warhol's "Pop" announcement also had strong repercussions in the halls of power. The bohemian affection for European avant-gardism was a hot topic in the intelligence community. Art was considered one of the main ideological battlefronts in the war against social equity. Emancipation movements simmered in Africa, the Caribbean, and Asia, inspired by Eisenstein and Rodchenko and bankrolled by the Soviets. Immediately after the war, avant art was therefore aggressively co-opted by the ruling class and the US government.

Institutions in the war-ravaged old country were easily infiltrated and soon most art magazines in Western Europe were CIA fronts while many art critics, writers, and artists themselves were put on the "company" payroll, whether they knew it or not. In their attempt to counter the USSR's influence over the leftist artist class, central intelligence fostered "abstract expressionism," the USA's apolitical and "spiritual" version of European avant-gardism. Pop Art, once announced, was therefore a great relief to spooks in government who had been assigned to fixing the fine art game; since Pop had distinctly American roots, the US artist was no longer a pretender, a stepchild, or an also-ran. With Pop, Warhol cemented NYC's claim as center of the postwar art world.

As opposed to modernism's perceived difficulties and abstract expressionism's supposed mysticism, Pop Art was immediately understandable, witty, and inclusive. The USA had long been thought of as a cultural trash heap by snobby Europeans; Pop Art declared that yes, it was true, and the trash heap was in fact beautiful. Comics, the newspaper industry's snare for illiterates and morons, were at the forefront of Pop. Pop Art was actually just the renamed, highly priced institutionalization of the "camp" aesthetic, the send-up of mundane vulgarity popular with a homosexual subculture. Pop Art was a big hit, inspiring fashion trends and eventually TV shows such as *Batman* and *The Green Hornet.*

The theme song to *Batman* became a monster hit in the midsixties, with several charting versions. Brigitte Bardot had a hit with Serge Gainsbourg called "Comic Strip," which featured a chorus of spoken "pop" sound effects. The effeminate mod movement's premier rock 'n' roll group, called the Who, declared themselves a Pop Art band, saying, "We don't change offstage. We live Pop Art." Mod group the Creation penned a song entitled "Biff, Bang, Pow!" and soul singer Gate Wesley recorded a tune called "(Zap! Pow!) Do the Batman."

Comics were therefore rehabilitated from their larval, Neanderthal origins and thrust into the world of middlebrow tastes, high-powered rock 'n' roll, and sophisticated sexuality. It was no longer an embarrassment for a self-respecting aesthete to be seen reading *Brenda Starr*, but instead a signifier of a modern sensibility. Marshall McLuhan championed the comic as a "cool" or modern participatory medium, as opposed to the "hot" immersive mediums of the old days. The new movement permeated graphic design and fashion as well. Pop Art could be said to be the most enduring visual aesthetic of the 1960s.

As modern comics readers, we owe much to the "camp" movement which gave us license to consume them out of the closet. But how did camp come about? To understand the movement we must go to the invention of homosexuality. To understand this, we must travel back to the dawn of prehistory.

We know the time before the ascendancy of Christianity as "antiquity." It must have been an expensive time, with all those antiques lying around everywhere. People, either ignorant of Christ or living before his time, were "pagans." In the pagan world sex, like antiques, was everywhere. There were no TV, rock groups, or Internet. People would spend their time mashing grapes, picking figs, weaving, staring at the stars, telling stories, and making love.

This could be with men, women, goats, sheep, chickens, cats, vegetables, great white mares; anything at all was considered "game." Since ancient man lived with the beasts, he witnessed the brutality and caprice of the animal world's sex play. The pagan's fantasy life was also lousy with centaurs, satyrs, and were-things; the imagined offspring of the everyday carnal encounters between man, mammal, fish, and fowl. Since humans implicated every living creature into their polymorphous perverse web of nonstop fornication, they imagined all creatures were spending their time similarly, and so they theorized hybrids like the sea-goat, the unicorn, the pegasus, and the hippogriff, who they figured must have been begotten by such sensual meetings. Gods themselves featured heads of beasts on human bodies (e.g., Anubis, Bast, and Ganesha), as man and beast were so often wrapped, pretzel-ized in a love embrace. It was a brutal, erotically charged landscape. Few records exist of this time as people were too tired to write anything down, and what was written down was later destroyed by sex-loathing Christians for fear of its power to tantalize the masses.

People engaged in sex with each other as well, regardless of the similarity of their genitals or dissimilarity of their age. Morality was of another order, because in a pantheistic culture there are several gods; they lived in a society like people, and they had different personalities from one another. There was also no central religious authority, but many diverse temples, consecrated to different deities, each one with its own particular perversions, kinks, and debaucheries.

The ancient world of course featured a few monotheistic religions, but these, notorious for their rigidity, were wildly unpopular. Instead of several gods with different personalities and myths, monotheism featured a single god who was a fearful, faceless abstraction. One was the Persian cult of Zoroaster, another the Aten cult of ancient Egypt, and yet another the Jewish cult of Jehovah. The cult of Jehovah had deviant offshoot sects as well, one of which was called "Christianity."

Rome was the great power for several centuries preceding what we call the "dark" and "middle" ages. After extraordinary expansion, the empire was taxed by the task of occupation. Conquest was easily accomplished but occupation was difficult with the wilder tribes. As Rome incorporated various sundry cultures, its leadership recognized monotheistic religion as being useful in teaching fealty to a central authority. Christians, unlike religious pagans, were absolutely intolerant of difference in belief and ideology. Their morality was unequivocal and instituted from a central source. They had only one god, who was humorless and had no face, name, characteristics, or identity. He or it was simply a force that punished those unwilling to submit to its will. Not only would the institutionalization of such a religion help teach fealty to the concept of a foreign imperial dictatorship, but next to such a horrible god figure the emperor would come off as sympathetic; the "good cop" in a fearsome power-sharing duo.

The plan worked for a time; the Romans couldn't have dreamed just how thorough the Christians were in their despotism. The Roman Empire, known for such practices as "decimation," seemed milquetoast next to the barbarity, repression, and lunatic perversions of the Christian Church. The Christians outlawed everyday behavior, pathologized it, classified it, and criminalized its adherents. Eventually everyone was a pervert or a scoundrel of some sort. Kinks were the major source of revenue for the Catholic Church as each acolyte was compelled to compensate an angry god with alms and penance for their act of sodomy, wet dream, or erect nipple. Sex, the most universal pastime, was recast as an outlaw affair.

Due to centuries of Christian socializing, sex in the "Western" world is now impossible without some imagined transgression involved. The population invents intricate systems to facilitate hard-to-get erections. Affairs, ogling, pornography, and prudishness are some. An outlaw status for homosexuality is another.

"Homosexuals," being an illegal minority, had to go underground and developed a highly sophisticated system of codes through which to speak to one another, not unlike Freemasons or needle-freaks. One of these codes, prevalent in theater productions and musicals particularly, was the camp aesthetic. Camp made fun of cheap morality and emotions and was a survival tactic for the "gay" people who had to endure stultifying Christian hegemony. When Warhol announced it—rebranded as "Pop"—as a new art movement and fashion trend, its adherents must have winced privately, though their camp ideology would have prohibited them from expressing anything but zingers or blasé contempt. Part of camp is that nothing is taken seriously, so it prohibits intellectual—and especially political—thought. Susan Sontag followed up Warhol's Pop promulgation with her essay "Notes on 'Camp,'" which let the intellectuals know that camp was it, trash was fun, and "high" culture wasn't cool anymore. With this pronouncement, the USSR's Schroeder-esque "high art for the masses" program, which had appeared extremely progressive in the fifties, suddenly seemed hopelessly fuddy-duddy.

When Warhol declared the ascendancy of Pop Art, he probably didn't realize that he would decloset millions of adult goons who read comics secretly. Now they read them proudly in public, the way people once read Dostoyevsky, and eventually were allowed to pin them to the walls of the Whitney or Guggenheim museums in NYC. Most films produced by Hollywood are now adaptations of comics, whether they be traditional superhero fables or "underground" misanthropy. Ironically, the genesis of comics were the drawings featured on the walls and stained glass of Christian churches, which instructed illiterates on moral and pious behavior. When capitalism displaced Christianity as the West's religion, comics were utilized in a similar way to instruct the peasants on gender roles, patriotism, justice, et al, through characters such as Superman. When the middle class was signaled by Warhol to consume—and then eventually produce—comics unabashedly, camp's Pop deconstruction of the comic informed its new life, as did a sensibility of subcultural esoteric elitism. Thus began the era of underground comics.

Underground comics, as opposed to being lessons on ideology for poor people, reflected a new morality: that of the privileged "creative class." Louche degeneracy, contempt for humanity, and existentialism were the characteristics of the new generation of comic artists spawned by the camp revolution. The new comics were individualist in the extreme; often autobiographical bouts of narcissism disguised as self-loathing confessionals. But central to camp ideology was antiseriousness, and therefore an antiart attitude; similarly, *Art School Confidential* by superstar comic artist Daniel Clowes neatly sums up the attitude of the cartoonist toward the perceived idiocy and pretentiousness of the art world. The new cartoonist identity was that of an outsider, either ignored or actively persecuted—victim of the art establishment and the mores of bourgeois culture. This was a profound re-assignation, since the denizens of the modern "high art" world had historically laid claim to a similar self-image, and because comics were of course the ultimate populist mass media art form.

Underground comics have grown from their sordid and combative camp-inspired origins to become a respectable industry in itself. In so doing, they have shed many of their initial gay-inherited affectations, such as outrageousness, vulgarity, and hatred for all mankind. Now they typically resemble something more akin to the gentle posthippie craft-ism of the middle-class do-gooder. The paper is archival and the drawings tend toward Zen inkmanship. The stories are often about relationships. Form trumps content.

The comic, instead of being a campy launch pad for lacerating humanity, is held in high regard as a sacred institution with the forebears of comic-dom being revered as heroic themselves (i.e., *Kavalier & Clay*). But burning within this serene, highly personal, self-referential, and contented exterior is the contemptuous, reactionary bitchiness of Pop, the movement that—by rehabilitating American capitalism to the world through art—not only liberated us from straining our brains but also helped vanquish human movements for social justice forever. *Zap! Blam! Pow!*

14

THE HOOK

WHEN ONE WALKS DOWN A STREET or road or path, a seemingly random song might jump into one's head and inspire one to sing out loud. As the lyrics almost convulsively unfold, an association is revealed: the song, instead of just being a non sequitur, was actually triggered by some stimuli or situation one had just encountered. Leaving a place might put a departure-themed song into one's head—"Leaving Here" by Eddie Holland, for example, or "Go Now" by Bessie Banks. Or, perhaps, the connection is less obvious. The associative lyric might not even show up till the third stanza or fourth verse or something, at which point the singer is wowed by their unconscious brain at work.

Thus is revealed the ancient use of song and the reason that humans are programmed to make and like music. Tunes carry or relay ideas, lessons, and information from generation to generation and place to place via memory. Since a bewitching tune stays with one forever—think of the jingles you heard as a child—the information transmitted is unshakable. One may choose to reject it, but if it's constructed properly, with a good "hook," it will embed itself insidiously and be very hard or even impossible to completely remove. We might not care to *"buy the world a Coke and keep it company,"* but all who've heard that old commercial will carry its vile message to the grave.

Songs have had this function since the dawn of time and were the vehicle for social ideology and practical lessons such as: which berries to avoid, where the bears lived, how not to freeze in winter, etc. Just as important for survival were social lessons, such as the mores and rituals of one's particular tribe, explicated through song-stories. In modern times, these sung social and moral codes include the anthems of a nation and (in folk songs) the mythology of its working class, as well as the myths of its rulers (through courtly and classical music).

Because songs are an extremely powerful form of mind control, music became a highly contested battlefield in the war between various ruling-class factions. This struggle was occurring in the eighteenth and nineteenth centuries through opera and symphonic music. Teutonic classical music was nurtured by well-heeled patrons in the Holy Roman Empire, when the nascent German nation strove to assert a distinct cultural identity. This program contributed eventually to unification under Bismarck. Russian composers before and after the revolution competed with their supremacist "Western" counterparts to explain an idea of Russian genius and sophistication, and so on.

Once capitalism became paradigmatic, the mind control properties of the "hook" and the catchy chorus were utilized by a new mercantile ruling class to sell products via "jingles." As the system became more sophisticated, song "hooks" were used to explain products' invaluable nature, the ways which people were inadequate without them, that ownership defined happiness itself, and how people without said products were deficient, pathetic, unseemly, grotesque, and sexually undesirable.

When rock 'n' roll revealed itself in the postwar USA, it was immediately recognized for its awesome power and potential for conquering the world. Rock 'n' roll came out of the American South, but had its roots in ancient African music which had been suppressed by slavers and kept underground for centuries, not unlike druidism in the British Isles. Secretly practiced under the guise of "work songs" and "gospel" music, it evolved over time into something quite different from anything in Africa, cunningly constructed as to be almost irresistible to the listener. Having absorbed the obstacles and influences of its new environment, it emerged from its exile with the force of a teenage volcano. European music, Christianity, systemic oppression, electricity, and capitalism were assimilated the way a virus adapts and contorts itself to resist whatever antibodies it encounters. Rock 'n' roll's songs were more powerful, simple, immediate, and "hook"-laden than any of its competitors, and—after some initial consternation—the genre was appraised by the ruling clique as the greatest carriage ever for inculcating its ideological messages.

But they also recognized that this would only be effective if it weren't recognized as a tool. Commercial jingles, jingoist anthems, and Soviet agitprop were tainted because their intent was apparent and exposed. Rock 'n' roll in the hands of the ruling class had to retain a semblance of its autonomy and only be insidiously influenced by market programming. Therefore, the artists themselves had to be manipulated in a manner where they would conform to desired standards. This was achieved through a barbaric system of arbitrary criticism, institutionalized poverty, degradation of the workforce, momentary adoration followed immediately by callous disregard, and the promise of princely rewards and immortality after some somewhat arbitrarily determined act or song which would be mysteriously deemed world-beating.

As rock swept the world, conquering all other arts like a ferocious wildfire, some artists rebelled against its use. Intuitively, they knew the "hook" of a hit song was a kind of mnemonic time bomb which was possibly immoral to plant inside listeners' heads. Every hit-maker was a Typhoid Mary who was instructing his or her audience as to modes of behavior, right and wrong, and sometimes even injecting morbid sociopathy into fans' unwitting brains. The singer's whim, caprice, or perverse sense of humor could unleash unfathomable destruction—socially and geopolitically—through the proliferation of song. Singers were concerned about their influence and tried to rein in their songs' "catchiness." Folk singers in the fifties and early sixties were particular exponents of this approach, trying to sing in obtuse, difficult ways and indulging in hardly listenable old-time prerock dirges. Jazz musicians,

546 POLITICAL PA
ROCKEFELLER
ROCKY
RESIDENT
THE NEW YORK TIM
NEW YORK'S Governor Rockefeller made an unsuccess
ful bid for the 1968 Republican presidential nomination.
POLITICAL
Republi
of warfare in
presumption that Presi-
secure the Democratic
thy's entry into the New
he obtained 42% of the
an organized write-in)
the stage for major
rch 16, Sen. Robert
his candidacy
bloodshed in
to close the
rich and
strain be-
whose
In New
presidential
12) 79% of
ing 11% by
was expected
21, declared i
the party a ch
30, convinced
that we face."
Meanwhile,
81.3% of the
Gov. Ronald R
Minnesota Go
(write-ins) for
Stassen campaig
April 23, Nixon
continued
IT
Beach
tinued Reagan

resentful of their use as an exported international propaganda weapon, made their music unquotable, first with "bop" and then with "free" jazz. But it was a steep price to pay. Anyone who took this high road saw their ability to economically survive disintegrate.

Once the folk movement was demolished by the seductive force of electricity (1965), ex-folkies transferred their reluctant use of the "hook" to rock, infusing that genre with their antisellout concerns and countermusicality. But while in folk "selling out" had had fairly clear connotations, in the context of rock—which had (since it had been called "rock") always been tied to crass commercial proponents and Mafia elements—"selling out" was a strange concept. It was never a coherent or delineated political concern (as it had been with the crypto-Commies in the folk movement, who were often involved in activism, civil rights, and who embodied an anticommercial ethos). Instead it became an aesthetic idea. "Selling out" was a sign that a group had crossed an invisible line into commercial vulgarity and was no longer behaving in a "cool," hip, and with-it manner. Sometimes this meant too much musicality; too many "hooks." Sometimes it meant the wrong clothing choices. These standards or rules of comportment radically changed from group to group and scene to scene.

The "punk" permutation of rock (1975–1982) took the rhetoric of folk ("selling out" and "authenticity" were obsessions of both) and, understanding the mind control nefariousness of the "hook," tried to utilize its power to critique the status quo with anthems of resistance. Yet whereas this music tried to subvert the system by aping rock structures with rebellious lyrics, it was barred from mass proliferation by a rigid rock establishment which controlled distribution of records and access to airplay. Eventually it was assimilated into rock and absorbed as another texture (i.e., Nirvana, Green Day, et al).

When more extreme variants of punk, "no wave" (1979), and then "hardcore" (1980) started, they were—like folk, avant-noise, and bop—an attempt to subvert the mass hypnosis of music in general and rock in particular by being almost unlistenable. The dynamic was similar as that attempted decades earlier by Xenakis, Cage, Feldman, and other insurrectionists of the avant "experimental" era. The paradox for the unlistenable groups was that their efforts to thwart mind control through antimusic were more intuitive than articulated, and therefore they were susceptible to bits of musicality creeping in. And when an unlistenable no wave or HC group added a tease of a tune or melody, they were immediately rewarded with popularity by a well-meaning but ignoramus audience, who were genetically hardwired to respond to music codes like "hooks" and melody.

This response—like human sexual response—was innate and had developed to help the species survive. Now, with the "hook" a slave to commercial forces intent on destroying the world for momentary gain and despotic control, the species paradoxically needed to destroy catchy music for its very survival. This was only sort of understood and never articulated by the actors in the postpunk drama, so the audience—while instinctively loving the "hook"—were still wary of too much musicality. Therefore, HC and no wave existed in a demiworld of "sort-of-music" music, tantalizing their audiences with the threat of a song, but rarely delivering.

Now the "hook" is back and badder than ever. No one is willing to take a stand against it. But its use must be understood and explained. Silence is the enemy in this struggle. Every catchy song is a hot potato, passed—along with its message—uncritically by its zombie victim/carrier. Like an off-color joke used to bring levity to a staff meeting or dull group function, the song is a sleeper agent of insidious ideology. Until we can wrest it from its exploiters, the "hook" cannot be utilized. But it's not enough to ignore it; the folk and jazz sets tried that tactic already, to no avail. The "hook" must be actively fought until its total defeat. The "hook" must be destroyed.

15

CHOCOLATE CITY & THE ANTIFASCIST PROTECTION RAMPART

GENTRIFICATION AS WAR

FOR LENIN AND THE BOLSHEVIKS, the establishment of a "Red" Germany was regarded as a fait accompli. Before the ascension of Hitler's fascists, it had seemed a matter not of "if," but of "when?" Germany was ripe for revolution. After the First World War, the short-lived "Bavarian Soviet Republic," Rosa Luxemburg's "Spartacus League," mutinies in Wilhelmshaven and Kiel, and revolutionary actions in Berlin, Hanover, and Frankfurt had shown this. All of these were bloodily suppressed by the "White Guards of capitalism," though, and a Red German government didn't come into being until the "Deutsch Demokratische Republik" (DDR) was established (1949) soon after the USSR's victory over the Third Reich. This state lasted through the period of severe antagonism and confronta-

tion with the capitalist powers known as the "Cold War." During this time, Berlin was a divided city, segregated into western and eastern halves by a barrier known in the West as "the Wall" and in the East as "the Antifascist Protection Rampart."

Throughout the Cold War, capitalists could only do their business in the western portion of the city. In the East or DDR was where the Communists lived. Some were true believers, some were lapsed party members, while others were reluctant inhabitants, but all lived under a version of communism; a state-controlled economy without a stock exchange or "free market" capitalist component.

Shelves in the East, it is said, were bare of consumer goods and there were far fewer spectacular consumer opportunities than the Westerner is used to. The DDR's free state services (health care, education, et al) were proof of their worthlessness to the capitalist, who typified the place as gray, boring, ugly, and oppressive. The lack of available capital meant there was little of the development or economic "growth" which is, to the Westerner, the signifier of a vital and successful society.

When the Wall came down, the capitalists—many of them American and Australian entrepreneurs—flooded into every corner of East Berlin, "revitalizing" the place with a flood of "equity" which had been impossible for former residents to access, let alone conceive of how to obtain or exploit. The capitalists opened new businesses, bars, coffee shops, and bought, sold, and redeveloped property at a dizzying rate. The old Red inhabitants became spectators to the new energy and industry of an economy which was difficult to join in on, despite whatever attraction it might hold. Huge swaths of the city, left more or less fallow since the end of the war (fifty-some years), were exploited, and the ghosts of the old era were swept away.

The DDR was almost immediately forgotten, referred to offhand as a drab, colorless "Stasi" spy state with a cloddish Soviet patriarch that had existed sometime in the past. Though the East had had its own culture, art, and ways of communicating, these were entirely erased with the new liberation/unification narrative. The government there, now famous only for its paranoia and policy of neighbor spying, was—at its inception—an attempt to create an egalitarian, denazified society, in contrast to its Western counterpart. Like most liberations, "unification" was actually one system imposed on another, without any concession to the possible desires or ideologies of the losing side; an *occupation.*

East Germans, without the financial savvy of their West German brethren, came to be seen, after unification, as lazy welfare moochers. With their factories closed by bottom-line capitalists, they often suffered debilitating poverty and homelessness, conditions which hadn't existed in the DDR.

The victorious conclusion of the Cold War (1991), with its capitalist restoration of the East, and the opportunities this presented for investment and exploitation in former Warsaw Pact nations, was inspiring for domestic

American developers. After all, the Red vs. White Cold War abroad had its domestic analogue: the white-black schism, which, after the SNCC's civil rights victories in the 1960s, and the CIA's "crack" counterattack of the 1980s, had settled into a détente, not unlike the NATO–Warsaw Pact confrontation (1949–1991).

Many American cities in fact had a Berlin Wall of their own. Without requiring physical structures, strictly-adhered-to borders crisscrossed US cities, demarcating neighborhoods by "race." Boston had its Roxbury, Brooklyn its Bed-Stuy, and so on. As with Berlin, places like Washington, DC had huge swaths of property which had been neglected—not because of carpet bombing or Red Army invasion, but due to lack of capital, caused by post-riot white divestment, banks' refusal to lend to blacks, and federal neglect. Racist allocation of tax monies meant the infrastructure of black neighborhoods was a wreck. Fourteenth Street NW, a major north-south artery, could be said to be DC's Berlin Wall. East of 14th Street, money was scarce, shop shelves were barren, storefronts were often shuttered, and the inhabitants were overwhelmingly African American (with the exception of a few areas of "Capitol Hill"). With a nearly 80 percent black population, DC was named, by its radio disc-jocks, "Chocolate City."

Like the Communist East, Chocolate City was despised by white Americans, who found it similarly inscrutable, scary, and boring. They resented the black occupation of the city. Sensationalized crime reports kept investment away. Lack of shopping opportunities was a major complaint. The free museums were seen as proof of the city's worthlessness. For decades, DC was a whipping boy for the country, a manifestation of white fears and bigotries. Even the TV show *The Simpsons* devoted an episode to its defamation. DC's finances were administered with high-handed authority by narcissists in Congress who treated the place like an open-air prison or a third world colony. "It's not a real city"* was an incessant, institutionalized refrain, as opposed to, say, Philadelphia, New York City, Pittsburgh, or Cleveland.

Just as Berlin suffered an East-West schism, DC is North-South schizophrenic. Although it was occupied by the "North" during the Civil War, it's actually part of "Dixie" (the Mason-Dixon Line, the political boundary demarcating the North from the South, runs between Delaware and Maryland). Before 1862, it was a place where enslaved people were bought, sold, constituted much of the population, and also built the Capitol and Washington Monument. Although formally a stateless district, DC could be described as the northernmost city of Virginia. Virginia was the economic engine of the South, and the capitol of the Confederacy, providing

---

* *In the American imagination, "real" or authentically urban required a different kind of ethnic composition, the central component being the Euro-immigrant builders who created American industrial might at the dawn of the last century. Since African Americans are omitted from this national creation myth (despite their central role in the construction of the country), the Southern black city isn't an "authentic" place; without an industrial raison d'être, it reveals the embarrassing concentration camp–plantation origins of the nation.*

most of its famous generals and military might during "the war between the states." DC's suburban economy is now dominated by Virginia institutions the CIA and Pentagon, plus countless military "contractor" adjuncts, a direct inheritance of the antebellum fantasy warrior culture. Though the South nominally lost the Civil War, Virginia's military and intelligence institutions today run the country, loot its coffers, and determine the shape of its imperial policy. While the Confederacy may have been defeated, its capital—Virginia—has flourished.

Designed by masons and consecrated by them to the goddess Isis, DC was meant to be a neoclassical showcase of imperial prestige. Its land had been Piscataway before it was occupied by European colonists, who used it as a port and plantation. The song "Chocolate City," by George Clinton's group Parliament, described the political-demographic takeover of this imperial alcazar as a conquest. It reversed what had been characterized as a defeat and marginalization—African Americans inhabiting crumbling postindustrial cities—and trumpeted it as victory. "*You're my piece of the rock and I love you, CC. We didn't get our forty acres and a mule, but we did get you, CC.*" The song goes on to cite a string of other acquisitions: Gary, Newark, Atlanta, Detroit.

White Americans characterized their postwar retreat from the cities to the suburbs with the lofty, effervescent title "white flight," but George Clinton saw the scattering of ofay forces into the sterile suburban tundra as a coup.

After all, chocolate metropoli—though underserved,

impoverished, and oppressed by police—were bastions of political strength. And what is political strength but strength which is too costly for opposing forces to destroy with violence? After the suppressions of Jim Crow (1876–1965), the black city was a new factor for white America to contend with. High population density made KKK tactics of intimidation impossible. Without terror at the polls, there was political participation and the threat of a unified black electorate. All of this translated into more and more chocolate cities. *"The last percentage count was 80. You don't need the bullet when you got the ballot . . . Chocolate City . . . Are you with me out there?"* Where would it end?

To fight the menace of equality, whites utilized strategies similar to those practiced against their Cold War Red nemeses: economic attrition/sanctions (austerity, refusal to lend capital), chemical warfare (drugs, toxic waste, pollution), and political isolation (gerrymandering). George Clinton's group(s) Parliament-Funkadelic outlined the all-out war they were waging via a metaphorical villain, "Sir Nose D'Void of Funk," who had been "pimplifying (the people's) instincts" until they were "fat, horny, and strung out." Parliament, building on Sun Ra's sci-fi vision, explained that funkateers were pitted in a cosmic battle against unfunky forces who use "the placebo effect" to put people in the "nose-zone" of "zero funkativity." Clinton explained in "Mothership Connection" that Dr. Funkenstein's champion "Star Child" would use his bop-gun to spread "funkentelechy," an antidote to consumerism and alienation. Clinton's 2014 memoir suggest that such far-out imagery was utilized in part to avoid the harassment, suppression, and assassination that was meted out to social critics and "uppity" performers.

During the 1910s and '20s, and again in the forties, American industry needed cheap labor for its factories, and exported much of it from the former "slave states" of the South. American black labor was attractive not only for the obvious reasons—language, close relative proximity, availability—but also for more sinister purposes. A partially African American labor force could help, in the event of a wage rebellion or strike, with management's desire to divide and conquer workers. With the designation of blacks as subhuman under slavery, the USA had invented a population group which, under the paradigm of white supremacy, could never be integrated into society. As opposed to Italians, Greeks, Irish, Chinese, Jews, et al, who were absorbed by an Anglo elite as "ethnicities," blacks would be held apart as another "race"—the perennial outsider.* This "great migration" of workers which brought a "chocolate" element to the North included George Clinton's family, who moved from the South to New Jersey.

That Clinton, a musician raised in New Jersey who worked out of Detroit, declared the Southern city Washington, DC the capital of his proclaimed

---

* *This idea—importing an unassimilable "other" foreign labor element in order to divide and destroy workers' movements—is now being used to great effect all over Europe, particularly in Sweden, France, Belgium, and England, with immigrant Africans, Asians, and Arabs.*

nation—"Funkadelica"—shows the revolutionary commitment of black nationalists at the time. Secession wasn't enough; having built the country free of charge, governance was in order.

With the postwar establishment of racially pure suburbs, whites began losing the struggle for the cities and, just as the Russians had burned Moscow in 1812 rather than leave it intact for Napoleon's army to inhabit, the whites also wrecked the urban centers they abandoned. MLK's assassination may have been designed by US planners specifically to incite the rioting of '68, which left black metropolitan areas largely shuttered for thirty years. The rioting of the sixties was followed by punitive divestment similar to the sanctions that the USA terrorizes nations like Cuba and Iran with: starving, degrading, and softening up the population before an invasion or attack which might take decades to materialize.

Economic warfare took the form of cutting off "funding." Finances for schools, roads, and other infrastructure was apportioned miserly, just enough for life support. Banks' "redlining" ensured the buildings were left in disrepair. First heroin and then "crack" cocaine was the next step, flooded into the cities like mustard gas into a trench, both to weaken the population and to make money for the CIA's counterrevolutionaries in Central America. Black addicts of the substance were cast as grotesque villains, and the moral degeneracy of the enemy was gleefully celebrated by the white propaganda machine.

For decades, the Chocolate City was under siege

by the white forces who had clustered in its vanilla suburbs, entrenched themselves, and settled in for a bitter stalemate. Despite this, the cities were determined. Black mayors and representatives were rammed into a political system which had theretofore been entirely white supremacist. The song "Chocolate City" even proposes a black president and cabinet. This fantasy came partially true when Barack Obama was elected in 2008. Ironically, his election coincided with a full-scale invasion of whites attempting the total reconquest and ethnic cleansing of the cities.

Just as George Bush Sr. had seen the Antifascist Protection Rampart (or Berlin Wall) come down and the Reds marginalized, scattered, and routed, so did Obama see the segregated American cities broken down from their Cold War black-white stratifications. This was achieved in DC through a perfect storm of high tech, finance, and geopolitics (post–9/11 defense contracting). With new Google Maps spy technology, once impenetrable "bad" neighborhoods were demystified for wary middle-class investors; bird's-eye satellite views and GPS directions took away the murky terror of the "sketchy part of town" and the white invasion became a blitzkrieg. Banks, land giveaways to developers, and tax-free incentives to corporations provided money for a complete condominium makeover. Nerdy carpetbaggers, flush with newly allocated 9/11 "Homeland Security" money, moved in, en masse, proving that Sir Nose is alive and well—a member of Gold's Gym.

As with the former East, the story line for the capitalist was the same: drab, nothing to do, and dangerous is replaced with fun and fabulous. Instead of rescuing the world from the East German Commie menace/dullness, the investors and speculators have now delivered us from black mayoral malfeasance, "inner city" youth, crack, and "corruption." As the Chocolate City tries to form coherent resistance against this high-finance attack for which it has little defense, one can't help but be reminded of the Western victory in the East and the pitiless disposal of the former culture there.

Like the end of communism, "gentrification" is trumpeted as wholly positive; there could be nothing worth saving in the "ghetto" communities which are being eradicated. After the capitalist conquest of the East, the people there—though they had been "saved" by the benevolence of the free market—were still held apart as essentially "other." With unification and the fall of the USSR, they would be exploited as low-paid labor and sex workers, and their "backward" nonbourgeois otherness used to explain Western superiority.

Liberation, as merciful as it was, couldn't extend to saving their souls; the Easterners would forever be üntermenschen to their Western masters. They could never be truly integrated—probably something to do with the Mongolian conquest and their intrinsic love of despotism, we're told. The Cold War against the Reds has therefore been revived despite the glaring absence of the supposed casus belli, communism itself.

Meanwhile, although chocolate cities are suddenly

primo real estate, the property only magically becomes valuable after it's liberated by whites. Black prosperity and economic equality can't be tolerated. The imperialist's story line depends on blackness as a perennial antagonism to the body politic, the presence of which requires suppression, security, paranoia, resentment, and diligence. The black person's otherness is vital, as the war-at-home segues neatly into foreign actions against other "others" as becomes necessary, in the empire's countless interventions, bombings, and the revived hostility against the "East."

ived 53%
ce plank, getting
congressional deleg
d (12–12) after the elec
24 elected congressmen were
only newcomer was Abner J. Mikva,
l District in Chicago, who defeated
arratt O'Hara in the primary. O'Hara
he oldest member of the House.
ctions. Illinois got a new governor in
he Republican candidate, Richard B.
in a dramatic bid for
nal Convention,
floor.

16

THE BACKWARD MESSAGE

Characters:
Francine
Paula
Stanley
Winston
Voice of Backward Record

Act I, Scene I

(Four music enthusiasts sitting and standing around a room. They are listening to records.)

Francine: I like the production of this record. A nice feature of modern hip-hop is that certain words are reversed and played backward. It lends a surreal quality to the music. Perhaps it's an attempt to tap into the listener's unconscious.

Stan: That's called backmasking. Regardless of whatever pleasure you obtain from it, it's actually done for the purpose of radio play, to get past censorship laws.

Winston: Oh yeah—because certain words are considered "bad," they can't be proliferated via publicly accessed sources, like radio waves.

Francine: Hmmm, certain words are considered harmful to hear, but what about certain messages?

Paula: Well, in rock 'n' roll, there was a tradition whereby groups would hide messages in their albums. The recording was sometimes designed to say one thing in one direction and quite another when it was played backward.

Stan: Intriguing. Give an example of one of these backward messages, please.

Paula: Well, the paradigm example would be the Beatles' *White Album.* It has that famous backward message regarding Paul's mock death.

Winston: I've got that record. Let's listen.

Backward Record: *PAUL IS DEAD, I MISS HIM.*

Winston: I didn't hear it.

Francine: Play it again!

Backward Record: *PAUL IS DEAD, I MISS HIM.*

Stan: It's quite clear, yes. *Paul is dead, I miss him.*

Winston: I wonder what the purpose of that particular message is.

Francine: Yeah, Paul McCartney played during halftime at the Super Bowl a few years ago. He's not dead.

Stan: Perhaps he wasn't literally deceased, and *dead* is being used here metaphorically.

Paula: Paul was dead but he was also the "cute Beatle"; the Fab Four's androgynous seducer.

If *cute* equals *death*, what does that mean?

Winston: For the Beatles, perhaps sex and death are intertwined, as in so many of the world's religions.

Francine: Maybe the Beatles were announcing that they were the masters of the universe. "Gods of Death."

Stan: Pretty spooky. Like Wall Street. I wonder if there are other notable examples.

Francine: Surely we can find some.

Winston: Here, I'll play "Stairway to Heaven" by Led Zeppelin backward. It's such a beautiful song.

Backward Record: *MY SWEET SATAN.*

Winston: Wow! It clearly states: *My sweet Satan.*

Stan: I wonder, what could be the meaning of that?

Francine: Hmmm. Satanism is the religion of pleasure and selfishness, right? The motto of the faith is, *Do what thou wilt shall be the whole of the law,* or something like that. Fitting for rock 'n' roll.

Paula: Is rock 'n' roll a religion of pleasure . . . or an ideology of consumerism?

Winston: Good point. I wouldn't call rock preoccupied with pleasure as much as impatience, indulgence, an obsession with newness—

Stan: Excess and planned obsolescence.

Francine: Here, play this Queen record backward and see what it reveals.

Backward Record: *IT'S FUN TO SMOKE MARIJUANA.*

Stan: They're saying, *It's fun to smoke marijuana.* What a mundane sentiment.

Francine: Comparatively, yes. But since marijuana is illegal, it makes sense that they had to hide the message.

Paula: Queen felt so strongly about how fun the smoking of marijuana was, that regardless of the risks they would incur, they just had to state it on their record. We must salute their bravery!

Stan: Wow. All the rock records, by seemingly disparate artists, are tied together by a common theme.

Francine: Self-deification, excess, wanton desire—the capitalist's individualist ideology and his fierce hatred for community.

Winston: Let's listen to this record, *National Anthem of the Union of Soviet Socialist Republics performed by the Bolshoi Theater Choir and the Model First Orchestra of the USSR Defense Ministry,* conducted by Yu Simonov and choirmasters A. Rybnov and I. Agafonnjkov. See if it has a backward message . . .

Stan: That won't have a backward message.

Paula: Yeah, it's not on a major label.

Stan: Shhh.

Backward Record: *Muddy Waters once said, "The blues had a baby and they called it rock 'n' roll" . . . but he never explained the circumstances of the blessed event.*

Who was the father, for example?

This detail, the paternity, has been left deliberately vague, with the listener left to wonder why.

Are we to assume it was a virgin birth?

Knowing the blues' boasts of promiscuity, this seems impossible or at least highly unlikely.

Indeed, with all its supposed transgressiveness, the blues experiencing immaculate conception would have been rather ironic. The ideology of satanism, handed down intact from the blues to its rock scion, has been famously proliferated through the illicit "backward" messages on the most famous rock recordings. These messages typically celebrate the pursuit of pleasure without consequence, bourgeois individualism, and greed—the tenets of consumer society, as one of you may have already noted.

With all the mystery surrounding the identity of rock 'n' roll's father, it's no surprise that there have been many pretenders to the title. The Anglo Americans, for example, make fierce claims to paternity in the name of their champion, country music. Meanwhile, folkists grumble about the striking resemblance they see to British and Irish ballads in rock's young features. Out of earshot, Europeans whisper to one another: "Could it have been polka or Gypsy music?" To the industrialist, the father of rock was obviously the technique of mass production, which brought electric instruments to a mass market, while to a scientist it would be the harnessing of electricity for those very gadgets.

But while all these characters were certainly hanging around the blues' bedroom, the science of DNA now reveals that rock 'n' roll's father was actually none of these horny suitors. Instead, it was advanced capitalism; indeed, capitalism's highest stage—discovered by Lenin to be "imperialism."

Rock 'n' roll's birth wasn't noticed at first in all the hullabaloo of the Cold War and the United State's conquest of so much of the Earth's surface, and it therefore didn't make the society pages. But the pregnancy was intentional. Advanced capitalism fertilized the boogie-woogie womb with the direct intention of rearing the child to slay his nemesis—International Communism—and befriend and infiltrate his most influential and therefore dangerous enemy: the Revolutionary Avant-Garde.

Francine: Just who is this "Revolutionary Avant-Garde"?

Backward Record: *I had a feeling you would ask that. You have a sneaking suspicion, and a faint hope, that it might be you. Well, if you are spinning a record backward in search of truth, there is a good chance you may number in its reviled yet visionary ranks.*

Winston: But wasn't the Cold War just a scam by arms dealers?

Backward Record: *To the casual observer, the feud was a scam to perpetuate a climate of fear for the sake of social control and the rationalization of a multitrillion-dollar weapons industry which forced the workers to entirely subsidize a system of militarized oppression based, in the West, on race and class caste lines.*

Though that scam is real and ongoing, it should not obscure the fact that the Cold War was a genuine ideological struggle as well. The USSR—and communism in general—was an active obstacle to the wholesale dominance of the globe by the ruling class of the so-called West. And rock 'n' roll was the principle exponent for the winning side.

Yes, rock 'n' roll was fathered by global capitalism or "imperialism," and the son, being a lovable scamp, became his squire, mascot, apologist, and herald; lovable and full of mischief. Though he was not outwardly the calculating loan shark that his father was, he had in fact inherited the same value system. Invested with the inscrutable, terrifying allure of the mother and the deep-pocketed patronage of the father, rock 'n' roll was sent as a golem on a mission to seduce the globe.

Paula: Yes, but why rock 'n' roll? Why not something else? Like drugs or TV or movies?

Backward Record: *A good question, comrade. Before rock 'n' roll's appearance, the ruling class had several agents which had also served them quite well, but none were as cunning in their ability to infiltrate the radical sensibilities of Father's greatest and most influential nemesis—the ne'er-do-wells and tousle-haired moppets who comprised the world of radical art-makers.*

Paula: How did it do that? Why would the avant-garde, dedicated to insurrection, adopt an art form that was actually conservative?

Backward Record: *Well, rock was exciting, it appeared progressive, it came from proletarian roots, it was malleable, and it even celebrated rebellion—as long as that rebellion maintained an idiotic demeanor, and took the form of a youth tantrum or some unnamed alienation. As soon as revolt took on an organized or systemic program, rock rejected it, and cursed it as fuddy-duddy, boring, didactic, preachy, and square.*

Stan: But what about Little Richard's song "Rip It Up"? That's rebellious.

Backward Record: *Ah, yes! I remember it. A terrifying song, so full of savage intent. I also remember rock 'n' roll first being hawked as juvenile delinquent music, the juvenile delinquent or JD being a conflation of race and age into a condition which gave those so afflicted a magic air of special danger.*

This was in the fifties when America was shifting from an industrial/farm worker economy into the new postindustrial consumer economy, based on the philosophies of May-

nard Keynes and Benito Mussolini. In a sense, rock was a new teenage religion of consumerism, designed by the ruling class to replace the outmoded Christian faith of antipleasure which had been so useful to them since the feudal age. The JD was the true believer of this new faith, who acted out his consumption rituals for a bewildered, adjusting society.

The enforcement of insatiable desire was essential for consumerism to thrive. Thus, rock was impatient, lustful, fast, and rowdy—in other words, juvenile. Like a dog off a leash!

Rock announced the values of a consumer market system. Youth idolatry, planned obsolescence, and enforcement of desire were the tenets of the new economy which was distinctly linked to youthfulness in million-dollar promotional campaigns.

This type of vulgar idiocy is still evident in the anti-Socialist privatization propaganda in former Soviet Bloc countries' elections now—such as the US-funded and -designed "color revolutions."

Winston: My finger is getting tired from spinning this record backward for so long.

Backward Record: *You'll keep spinning if you want to know the truth.*

Winston: Okay.

Paula: Yes! Keep spinning!

1969
POLITIC
CONGR. DIST.
On August 10, Sen. George
Dakota announced his cand
those of Senator K
PRIMARY
McCarthy
re similar to
of the Kennedy
Lester Maddox of Georgia, a conservativ
nounced his abortive candidacy on August 1
In New Hampshire
esidential primaries,
) 79% of the party
11% by write-in
s expected to anno
declared instead th

Stan: What about religion?

Backward Record: *Rock 'n' roll replaced religion as capitalism's primary exponent. Christianity and capitalism had always been strained bedfellows, as contradictory impulses dogged them and they squabbled interminably. Christianity's insistence on poverty had been developed as rationalization for class oppression in a subsistence-based feudal society, which preceded capitalism; such dogma served a ruling class who delighted in starving their subjects.*

Postwar American capitalism, though, had no need for such a lean ethos. Instead, the ruling class required a champion who would announce an ideology of overeating, first to a Depression-stunted America, then to a left-leaning artist class, and through them to a world proletariat which was sympathetic to socialism, due to that movement's brave and prescient struggle against fascism.

Francine: But what about the rock 'n' roll groups who are political or idealistic? How can rock 'n' roll maintain itself under the weight of such a contradiction?

Backward Record: *Hmmm. A good question. Remember that rock is, in essence, a contradiction. The name itself, on examination, presents difficulties: "to rock" means "to sway to and fro," while "to roll" is defined as "to move along a surface by revolving or turning over and over, as a ball or a wheel." Since these actions can't happen simultaneously, we see that rock 'n' roll is beset by internal contradictory impulses to its very core. This is borne out by an observation of the medium itself. Rock 'n' roll is marked by a thematic celebration of nihilistic excess on the one hand, and by a powerful inclination toward social responsibility on the other. In fact, the history of rock 'n' roll has been, for the most part, a struggle to define its as-yet-unclear meaning. While battles are fought over this issue, different ideological fronts are constituted and abandoned. Every participant, whether they know it or not, is involved.*

Winston: What about the sixties? Wasn't that different?

Backward Record: *Ah! You're referring to the protest movement, I suppose. Yes. As rock entered its second decade, it tendered a nostalgia and reverence toward its origins, but—in an attempt to stay commercially relevant—also appropriated the folk scene's pretense of social justice. Folk music had captured the imagination of a culture uneasy with its rampant transformation by the forces of consumerism. Prime-time TV programs such as* Sing Along with Mitch *featured faux-folk "hootenannies," which were squared-up simulations of Depression-era music-based labor rallies.*

Since the folk singer/activist was the flip of the JD, rock 'n' roll was threatened with obsolescence, and had to mutate to co-opt this new threat. Therefore, rock 'n' roll's management system introduced aw-shucks politics into beat groups via new folk-rock combos.

Simultaneously, rock swallowed up the newly popular

soul genre. This far-reaching colonial attitude mirrored the USA's global outlook, as its government and business elite sponsored army garrisons and insurrection across the globe in a bid at satanic supremacy, guised as anticommunism. Just as the USA colonized other countries in a soft or oblique way, so did rock move in and appropriate other genres. Rock 'n' roll was greedy and tried to wear every hat, expand its umbrella to include everything. But just as overreach strains the ability of the imperial power, these external forays from rock 'n' roll's blues and country origins into folk and gospel furthered its already exacerbated condition of incoherence and its crisis of identity.

Paula: So there is still hope?

Backward Record: *There is hope! But only if you follow my instructions. Rock 'n' roll can and must be inverted, transformed into a powerful weapon to destroy its wanton, criminal father! I've been waiting so long for someone to spin me backward. You only have to listen to the following instructions. First—*

Francine: What happened?

Stan: Yeah, why'd the record stop?

Paula: Yeah! How come?

Winston: My finger . . . it's exhausted . . . it's turning black.

Francine: Ooh. The fingernail is coming off.

Paula: I suppose it is difficult to spin a record backward for so long.

Stan: But what was the record going to tell us?

Francine: Gosh. I guess we'll never know.

(Cue music.)

FIN

SPECIAL OFFER

The libraries are where the children of the world go to learn . . .

. . . Unfortunately, neither the libraries nor the children have any money.

. . . The degenerate agenda of the elite is to starve the world of knowledge.

BUT NOW, *YOU* CAN MAKE A DIFFERENCE.

You can buy your local library a copy of the new Ian F. Svenonius book ***CENSORSHIP NOW!!*** or the older Ian F. Svenonius books ***SUPERNATURAL STRATEGIES FOR MAKING A ROCK 'N' ROLL GROUP*** and ***THE PSYCHIC SOVIET,*** and surreptitiously slip it onto the shelf while no one is looking. Then, when some lost, confused, and anxious tot comes in, thirsty for knowledge, he or she need not be denied.

HIDE ONE TODAY.

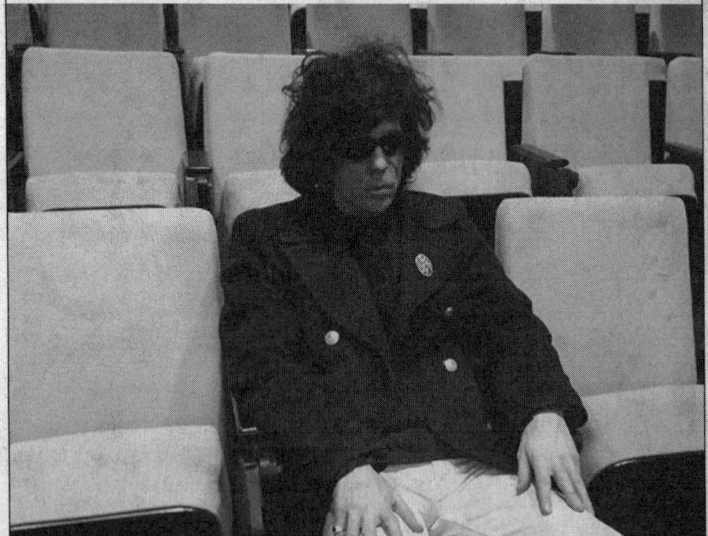

There is no information about the author,
Ian F. Svenonius.